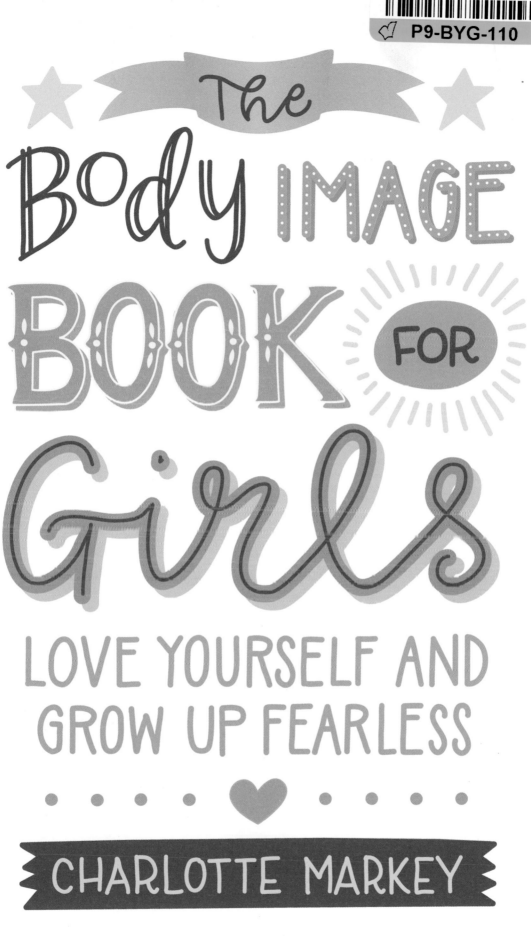

The Body Image Book for Girls

LOVE YOURSELF AND GROW UP FEARLESS

CHARLOTTE MARKEY

ILLUSTRATIONS BY TIM OLIVER

University Printing House, Cambridge CB2 8BS, United Kingdom

One Liberty Plaza, 20th Floor, New York, NY 10006, USA

477 Williamstown Road, Port Melbourne, VIC 3207, Australia

314–321, 3rd Floor, Plot 3, Splendor Forum, Jasola District Centre,
New Delhi – 110025, India

79 Anson Road, #06-04/06, Singapore 079906

Cambridge University Press is part of the University of Cambridge.
It furthers the University's mission by disseminating knowledge in the pursuit of
education, learning, and research at the highest international levels of excellence.

www.cambridge.org
Information on this title: www.cambridge.org/9781108718776
DOI: 10.1017/9781108752961

Cambridge University Press © 2021

First published 2021
3rd printing 2021

Printed in Singapore by Markono Print Media Pte Ltd.

A catalogue record for this publication is available from the British Library.

ISBN 978-1-108-71877-6 Paperback

Additional resources for this publication at TheBodyImageBookForGirls.com

DR. CHARLOTTE MARKEY

is a world-leading expert in body image research, having studied all things body image, eating behavior, and weight management for her entire adult life (over 25 years!). She is passionate about understanding what makes us feel good about our bodies and helping people to develop a healthy body image. Charlotte loves to share her body image wisdom with others and is an experienced book author, blogger, and professor at Rutgers University, Camden. She currently lives in Pennsylvania with her daughter, Grace, son, Charlie, husband, Dan, and their dog, Tobey. For fun, she likes to run, swim, travel, and read, but usually spends her free time driving her kids to see their friends and nagging them to clean their rooms.

To learn more about Charlotte Markey, you can visit her website at www.CharlotteMarkey.com or connect with her on Facebook (Dr. Charlotte Markey), Twitter (@char_markey), Instagram (char_markey), or YouTube (Body Positivity).

TABLE OF CONTENTS

CHAPTER 1

WHAT IS BODY IMAGE?

#BodyImageBasics

> Your body is an instrument, not an ornament.
>
> Lexie and Lindsay Kite, PhDs and co-founders of Beauty Redefined

Do you ever feel like you're too short (or too tall)? Do you ever wish that your hair was straight and not curly? Have you ever looked in the mirror and wished for longer legs? Do you wish your breasts were larger (or smaller)?

If you've ever had a **negative** thought about your appearance, you're not alone. Most girls and women would like to change at least one thing about how they look—if not many.

Even celebrities—the people we often think of as looking "perfect"—often struggle with concerns about their appearance.

Taylor Swift has admitted:
"I definitely have body issues, but everyone does."

Actress Reese Witherspoon has said:
"I have **cellulite**. I have **stretch marks**. I feel intimidated by Victoria's Secret."

Actress Ariel Winter claims:
"I had body insecurities when I was younger. I still do."

It's not just average people who think about their appearance and wish they could look different. It's almost everyone. The goal of this book is to help you develop a positive view of yourself. A **positive** view of yourself doesn't mean that you think you're better or more beautiful than everyone else. Reese Witherspoon said, "Hollywood is one of those endless competitions. But it's a race toward nothing. There's no winning. You're never going to win the pretty race." Your life isn't a beauty pageant. A positive view of yourself means learning to treasure and care for your body. You can succeed in this goal, and this book will help you.

> **IN THIS CHAPTER, YOU'LL LEARN**
>
> ○ how body image is defined,
> ○ why it's important to have a positive body image, and
> ○ why reading this book and working on developing a positive body image will improve your life in a variety of ways.

What is body image?

Body image is how you think and feel about your body. Obviously, the way you think and feel about your body—your body image—matters. For example, if you dislike your curly hair, you may spend a lot of time trying to straighten it. If you want to be taller, you may wear shoes with platform soles or high heels. If you really want your nose to be smaller, you may consider getting surgery to change the size or shape of it.

But what if there is a better way to think about your body? Maybe changing how you look isn't the answer. Maybe there is an easier way. **This book is full of information and advice about body image that will help you understand your body and develop positive feelings about it.** Most women I know (including myself) wish they'd had this sort of information when they were girls your age.

MY STORY

Alyssa Elizabeth, 15 years old

I think I started having some typical body image issues when I was about 12. I started worrying about looking stupid. I can still remember this one time when I was at summer camp, the summer before 8th grade. Everyone was wearing short shorts and crop tops, but I didn't want to. It was hot, but I knew that being that exposed would make me uncomfortable. But then I sorta realized that no one really cared what I wore one way or the other. I started to think about some of this differently—no one really notices a lot of the details of how I look. Who is going to remember? Who really cares? Everyone is probably thinking about themselves more than other people. When I realized that no one was judging each other, I tried to stop judging myself.

Not long ago I had a somewhat similar epiphany (or "ah ha!" moment). It seems so strange that I was born with this body—I was born this way. Why should I have to change myself to please other people? Some of my friends have had these thoughts, too. A lot of my friends are athletes and they have **muscular** bodies. They need those muscles to play lacrosse and soccer. They are great athletes and they work hard. I don't think any of us want to change ourselves, but we all want to feel accepted, and to feel good about ourselves.

I guess it's normal to not always feel confident. But I think it's important to try. My mom tells me that it's OK to fake it until you make it (about all sorts of things). You'll start to believe in yourself and be confident, but it can take time.

I guess if I had one thought to tell younger girls, it's that everybody is a little bit different. You don't have to be "one size fits all." You should be proud of yourself! Think: This is me.

Why I wrote this book

I have a daughter, and I want her and her friends to have this book and read it either on their own or with their moms, dads, sisters, cousins and friends. This book is full of helpful, **evidence-based information** that my daughter and her friends—and you and your friends—can turn to for answers to questions about body image and related topics, such as **nutrition** and **physical activity**.

Most moms worry about their kids, but sometimes I think it's worse as a parent when you know too much. I've been a **research scientist** studying eating **behaviors** and body image for more than 20 years now. When I think of my own kids (Grace is 12 and Charlie is 14 years old), I worry a lot. I know about all the mistakes people make, and I don't want my kids to make those mistakes. I don't want you to, either.

There is a lot of bad information available about the topics I cover in this book. This bad information is dangerous, and can lead to risky decisions. In fact, adults often don't do a good job of making sense of what to eat, how much to **exercise**, and when to go to sleep. This book can help you develop good habits while you're young—good habits will stick with you as you get older.

My hope is that this book will be a good resource as you become a teenager and young adult—that you'll read it from cover to cover, but also pick it up when you have a question about something and you want a factual answer. Sure, you can google all the topics I cover in this book, but you'll find a lot of misinformation and myths about body image on the internet. My goal is to provide you with scientific evidence about the issues I discuss, not just my opinions.

In each chapter, you'll find the following:

- **Reliable information:** I summarize the latest **science** on the topic. If you see a pink word you don't know, check the **glossary** in the back of this book. As you read, remember you're a member of a large community who cares about these issues. I don't know any women who haven't been concerned about these issues, and talking about them can be helpful and **empowering**.

- **Q&A:** During my career, I've talked with hundreds of girls. For this book, I've asked them what questions they have about their bodies, eating, exercising, and all the other topics in this book. I provide factual answers to their questions—which are probably the ones you have, too. Below is an example.

Q & A:

Are any of the pictures of people in magazines or online real?

A lot of the pictures that you see are actual people, but nearly all images are modified: one photographer I talked with estimated 99%. Photographs of famous, beautiful people are almost always altered to make them look prettier, younger, and thinner. It's easy to think that other people have perfect hair, bright eyes, no pimples, perfectly white teeth, long legs with no cellulite anywhere on them, and enviable noses, but they probably look a lot more like you in real life. If a professional photographer edited pictures of you, you'd look like a star, too! The next time you see a photo of a famous person, remember that the photo is edited.

- **Myths and misbeliefs:** In each chapter, I'll share "**myths** and **misbeliefs**" about body image and related topics and explain why they aren't true. Here is an example:

⭐ MYTHS AND MISBELIEFS

Telling people that they need to lose weight—"body shaming"—will motivate them to lose weight and look better.

There is no evidence that this is true! In fact, it seems that the opposite is true!

Maintaining a healthy weight (see Chapters 2 and 6 for more information about what a healthy weight might be for you) is important for maintaining good health. But making people feel bad about themselves is not "motivating." If you are concerned about a person's weight or health, the last thing you should do is try to make them feel bad about it. Instead, be a supportive friend and try to encourage people to eat well, exercise regularly, and avoid media and other influences that may make them anxious or upset about their weight.

- **My story:** In the process of writing this book, I've relied on scientific research that takes into account hundreds and thousands of girls' experiences. But I've also interviewed individual girls, like Alyssa Elizabeth (her story is earlier in this chapter). These girls are all between the ages of 14 and 23, and they shared their specific experiences in detail. Each chapter will highlight some of these real girls' experiences, in their own voices.

- **Inspiration:** When it comes to feeling good about our bodies, all girls and women can use some inspiration. Each chapter will contain quotes, illustrations, and bits of information to help you think about your body in a positive way—and maybe even laugh about some of these issues.

- **Find out more:** The information in this book is evidence-based and scientific in nature. In other words, it's not just my opinion, but based on thousands of scientists' research and understanding of body image and the other topics discussed. If you want to read more about a topic, these references will be a good place to look.

I want you to grow up to be strong, independent, and powerful. **Once you know the facts about the smartest way to encourage your positive body image, nothing will be able to hold you back!**

✓ SUMMING UP #BODYIMAGEBASICS

- ✓ Body image is defined as how you think and feel about your body.

- ✓ Your body image may affect your physical health, mental and emotional **well-being**, and your health behaviors.

- ✓ Understanding your body image and knowing how to develop a **positive body image** will benefit you across your entire life.

CHAPTER 2

YOUR CHANGING BODY

#TimeToGrowUp

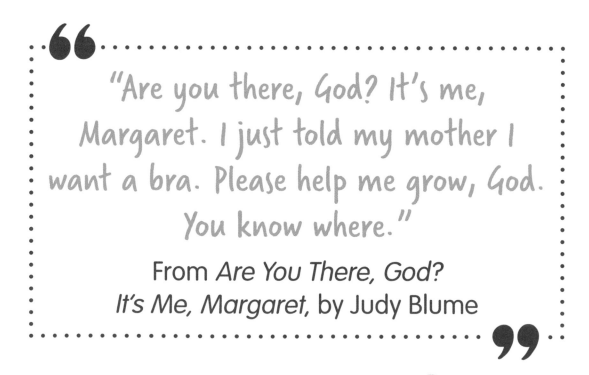

"Are you there, God? It's me, Margaret. I just told my mother I want a bra. Please help me grow, God. You know where."

From *Are You There, God? It's Me, Margaret*, by Judy Blume

What is puberty?

I'm sure you've heard the word **puberty**, but maybe you aren't sure exactly what it means. The word puberty comes from the Latin word *pubescere*, which means "to grow hairy." You probably already know (and maybe you've already experienced for yourself) that growing up does include getting hairier, but there's more to it than that.

IN THIS CHAPTER, YOU'LL LEARN

- about the changes you will experience during puberty,
- how puberty may affect your body image, and
- how to cope with the physical changes you experience during puberty and keep a positive view of yourself.

MY STORY

Abby Suzanne, 14 years old

I feel pretty good about my body most of the time. I guess sometimes I feel a bit awkward when I dance. I've been doing dance for a few years now, and it's hard not to be a bit **self-conscious** in that setting. I felt especially self-conscious about my body when I first got my period. I was earlier than my friends and it made me feel different from them. I wished I had someone to talk with about all of that. I knew it was normal and even a good thing, it just felt a little weird.

I guess I feel as good about myself as I do because I feel like my mom and my friends are with me every step of the way. It's important to have them to talk to. They tell me all of the good things about myself and that makes it easier to ignore what I see as the less-than-good things. I would definitely tell other girls to be sure they have someone they can talk to about their bodies, whether it be a mom, aunt, sister, friend, or even a teacher or something. We all seem to have body **insecurities** and have a hard time seeing ourselves objectively. Other people can be valuable in reminding us of our positive qualities.

What changes during puberty?

Skin

You've probably noticed that as kids become teenagers, they sometimes get pimples, or spots (**acne**). This is related to changes in your skin that all teens experience. It's normal for your skin to get rougher and dryer in some places, but also oilier in other places. This oiliness may lead you to break out and develop red bumps and patches on your skin. Pimples, or spots, can be a cause for concern or self-consciousness among teens, but in most cases they're treatable. Be sure to wash your face with a soap specifically intended for your face. These can be found in nearly any drugstore or grocery store. You may also want to treat pimples with a cream that contains **salicylic acid** or **benzoyl peroxide**. Both can cause your skin to get drier. If this doesn't help, you can ask your doctor (perhaps a **pediatrician**, or a **dermatologist**, a doctor that specializes in skin care) for a more powerful skin treatment.

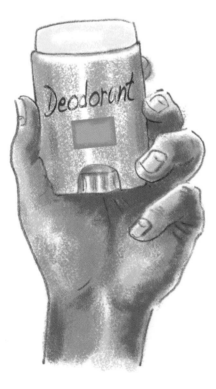

Changes in your skin also contribute to your likelihood of sweating more and smelling like **body odor** (BO) more often. Most of the sweat occurs under your arms where you have a lot of **sweat glands**, and deodorant can greatly help reduce the likelihood of smelling bad. If you don't like the smell of one particular deodorant, or if it doesn't seem to work for you, then try another kind. There are lots of options to consider.

Bones, heart and lungs

Even body parts that don't seem related to puberty are affected by it. For example, your bones grow in length (how do you think you get taller?) and they become thicker. Your skeleton will be about twice the weight at the end of puberty as you grow taller and your bones become stronger. Your heart also nearly doubles in size over the course of puberty. This allows your heart to beat more slowly while

MYTHS AND MISBELIEFS

Eating chocolate can cause you to break out.

It seems pretty unfair that something as delicious as chocolate could make you break out in spots or pimples. Fortunately, this is mostly a myth. I say "mostly" because scientists have found that what you eat can affect your skin. Eating **healthy** foods, including plenty of fruits and vegetables, can help your skin look healthier and prevent breakouts. Avoid eating a lot of sugar and simple carbohydrates ("carbs," found in white bread and other **processed foods** like chips or crisps) because these foods can increase the risk of getting acne. Acne is caused by the many changes occurring in the body during **adolescence**, so a healthy **diet** may not prevent acne.

still pumping blood as well as it did when you were younger. Your lungs also get much larger, which allows oxygen to move through your body more effectively. Overall, these physical changes can make you taller, bigger, and stronger. They can even make you more capable of doing well at a variety of sports.

Hair

Hair creeps up in all sorts of places when you go through puberty. This may be one of the first things you notice when you begin puberty. It may begin with a few hairs under your arms, or **pubic hair**, or hair on your legs, and maybe even on your face. Your hair also gets thicker and darker. Some of this new hair may be the same color as the hair on your head, but some may be a different color.

Often, girls and women will remove some of this newly appearing hair, but you absolutely do not have to do this. There are no health reasons for doing so and body hair is completely natural and normal. Ask women you

trust about this, whether it be your mom, an older sister, an aunt, or a grandma. (Of course you can talk to your friends about puberty, but friends may not always be as reliable and useful a resource as an older woman.)

If you decide to remove body hair, there are lots of ways to go about it; two of the most common are shaving and **waxing**. Each has its pros and cons. Shaving can remove unwanted body hair quickly, but it's easy to accidentally cut yourself with a razor, so be careful. Before shaving body hair, be sure to consult with someone or look for a helpful YouTube video. Hot wax is also used for body hair removal. Usually, a professional will apply wax to unwanted hair, and when the wax is removed, the hair is also.

Keep in mind that a desire to get rid of hair probably comes from what you've learned from the people and **media** around you. In some cultures, hair removal isn't part of growing up. It's primarily in western cultures that hair removal is common.

Breasts

A normal part of puberty for girls is **breast growth**. As you've probably noticed, some women have smaller breasts and some have larger breasts. You can't know how you're going to turn out until you've finished puberty, but your breasts will change at least a little bit. On average, breast development isn't finished for most girls until they're 16 or 17 years old.

Scientists and doctors tend to describe breast growth in five stages. Basically, the process of going from a child's to a woman's breasts involves changes in both the **nipple** (which gets bigger) and the tissue surrounding and underneath the nipple (which also gets bigger). Not every girl has the same experiences in terms of changes to their breasts. Changes may occur so slowly that you don't even realize they're happening, or they may occur so quickly that you grow out of shirts after a couple of months.

As your breasts grow, you will probably notice them more. Running, for example, can cause breasts to move up and down in a way that's new to you. Many girls and women use special underwear to support their breasts. This may be a fitted tank top, a "**cami**," or a bra. There are a lot of options, and you should find what's comfortable for you. Even if you don't feel like you need the support, you may feel more comfortable with an extra layer between your breasts and your shirts. If nothing else, this keeps the shape and outline of your breasts (and, specifically, your nipples) from being visible.

There are five stages of breast development, as shown on this page, which are often called "Tanner stages" after the doctor (James Tanner) who first identified them. These stages are used by doctors and researchers to identify breast development. (There are also five stages of development for girls' and boys' genital areas.)

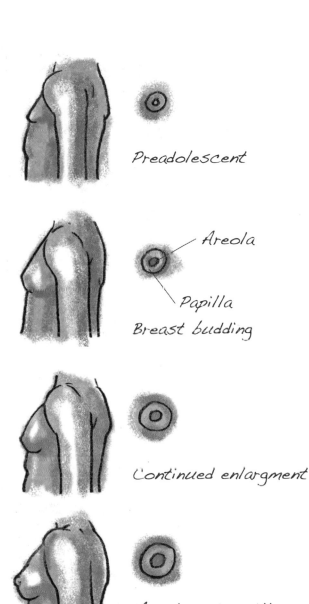

Preadolescent

Areola

Papilla

Breast budding

Continued enlargment

Areola and papilla form secondary mound

Mature female breasts

Q & A:

I feel like ever since I started to develop, people are looking at me differently. Even my aunt told me to cover myself up better the other day. She told me that boys will think I'm fast if I'm not careful about concealing my hips and breasts. I can't help it that I'm curvy, even though I'm only 12. Most of the women in my family have some serious curves—black women often do! That's just the way we are. Why do people make me feel like this is my fault?

Girls develop at different ages, and it's definitely not your fault that you're an early developer. Some research suggests that black girls do tend to develop earlier than white or Asian girls. It may be difficult to keep people from noticing your body, but that doesn't mean you should feel uncomfortable with who you are becoming. Your aunt most likely wants to protect you and has your best interests in mind. She doesn't want her young niece to be the focus of boys' or men's attention. Perhaps what's most important is that if you feel that a boy (or man) says something about your body that's inappropriate, or if someone touches you in a way that makes you uncomfortable, tell someone you trust right away! Talk to your aunt or an adult you feel comfortable with, even if that's a teacher or a coach. (See Chapter 3 for more information about harassment.)

Genitals

Genitals is the general name for the male and female reproductive body parts. Your **vagina** will also change during puberty. Unless you spend a lot of time looking at it with a mirror, you may not notice a lot of the changes that take place in your vagina. Some of the changes are hidden by the growth of **pubic hair** that will cover some of your vagina. (By the way, it's totally normal to be curious and get a mirror out to look.)

The primary changes in your vagina include growth of the **labia majora** and **labia minora**. These external organs are together referred to as the **vulva**. These parts help to cover up and protect the urethra (where urine comes out) and vaginal opening (where **menstrual blood** comes out; more on that below). The **clitoris** also grows during puberty; the clitoris is the primary source of female sexual pleasure. The color of the vagina also deepens so that what was once similar in color to the rest of your skin is now typically a darker color.

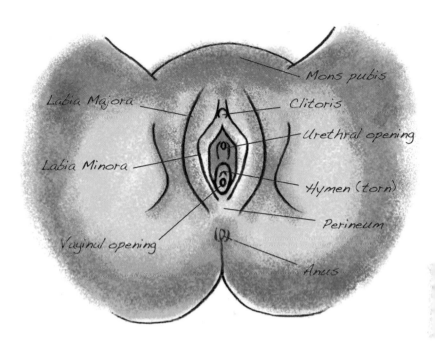

Mons pubis
Clitoris
Labia Majora
Urethral opening
Labia Minora
Hymen (torn)
Perineum
Vaginal opening
Anus

Hormones

Up until puberty, girls' and boys' **hormones** are very similar. This changes during puberty. At puberty, girls' levels of hormones, particularly female-specific hormones, increase dramatically.

Sometimes parents and other adults will say that the moodiness that develops during puberty is due to hormone changes. This may be partially true, but it's likely an overly simple explanation for a lot of the complicated changes that take place during puberty. For example, it's possible that you may feel hungry soon after eating, or tired despite sleeping a lot, due to changes in your hormones. In turn, hunger and fatigue may make you grouchy. Or maybe you feel **stressed** because you haven't been getting along with your friends at school and you don't have classes with the people you wish you did. Some of this may be related to your hormones, but a lot of it may not be.

The **bottom line** is that you shouldn't feel like your life is out of control due to hormone changes that you can't help. **Your hormones play a really important role in your development, but they don't control everything.**

MY STORY

Sophie Jane, 17 years old

It's a bit difficult for me to describe how I feel about my body because my feelings fluctuate. I think it's pretty common for girls my age, the ones I've talked to at least, to feel really self-conscious and to pick apart their appearance one day, and then to feel really amazing about themselves the next day. I think it's impossible to find a girl who feels great about her appearance 100% of the time. There are days where I look at myself in the mirror and only see the things that I don't like about my body. There used to be a lot more days where I felt like that, but I've reached a place emotionally where, even if I am having those intrusive negative thoughts about my body, I'm at least aware that those thoughts aren't accurate and I don't let them affect me as much.

One thing that's really affected my attitude toward my body is my interest in fashion. It's been both good and bad for me because, on the one hand, I do worry about how my body looks in the clothes that I'm wearing, but on the other hand, I now know how to dress in a way that makes me look good and feel confident. By developing a personal style that isn't based on what most girls (whose bodies typically look a lot different from mine) are wearing or what's trendy, I've learned to appreciate my body a lot more. There are certain things that I, a 5' 9" inch girl, can pull off that shorter girls can't, and vice versa, and I've learned to accept that.

Going through puberty definitely impacted how I felt about my body. Puberty is an awkward time for everyone, including me. To sum up my puberty experience, I grew up before I grew out. So, when I turned 14, I was 5' 9", weighed about 120 pounds and looked like an uncooked stick of linguini. I was thrilled when, about a year later, my hips got a bit wider, my legs looked more shapely, and my breasts were able to fill out my shirts.

My friends have influenced how I feel about my body significantly. I am really lucky to be friends with girls who don't judge or make fun of other girls' bodies. There were other groups of girls that I go to high school with who would feed each other's insecurities. If any of my friends expresses an insecurity about their body, the rest of us are quick to tell them that they're beautiful and that there is no reason for them to change a thing, whereas girls in other groups would encourage each other to try fad diets or to over-exercise. I can't even imagine how messed up my perception of my body would be if I had friends like that.

My mom has also been influential when it comes to my body image. She doesn't make critical comments about my body, and she's tall, too, so she understands the struggle of finding pants that are long enough. There are tons of people that I've never even met who influence me as well. Because of **social media**, I am exposed to pictures of girls with perfect hair, perfect make-up, and perfect bodies on a daily basis. It can be really hard not to compare yourself to them. I definitely do at times, and I know it's **unhealthy**.

If I were to give advice to other girls about body image, it would be to talk about it with other girls as much as possible. By talking about it with girls that you love and trust, you can build an emotional support system and realize that you're not alone and that other girls feel the same way that you do about your body. It can be easy to assume that other girls who you think are prettier than you have no insecurities, but those same girls are probably looking at you and thinking the same thing.

I think that body image is a "grass is always greener" type of thing. For example, girls who are skinny are envious of curvier girls because they think curvier girls look sexier and look better in low-cut tops and tight skirts, but curvy girls are envious of skinnier girls because they think that skinnier girls look more like models and look better in short shorts and crop tops. Girls assume that if they had a "perfect" body, they would be happy all the time, and that's just not true. Although crash dieting and exercising way too much may seem like the best way to gain confidence, it definitely is not. Real confidence comes from a healthy body image and that can be achieved no matter what you look like. It's not easy, but as long as you surround yourself with people who know that you're beautiful, you'll have a healthier body image.

Menstruation

Menstruating, or getting your **menstrual period** (aka your period), is a pretty big deal. Some girls worry because they don't know when it's going to happen for the first time. You may feel excited to get your period, or you may feel worried about this change. Either way, it's important to understand what your period is and what you can do to prepare for it.

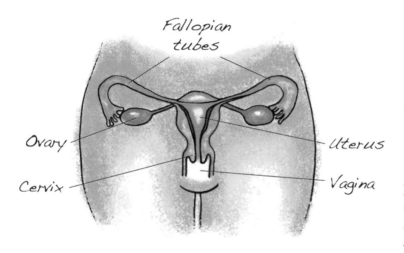

At some point during puberty, your body will start to prepare for the day when you may want to have a baby. Don't worry! You probably don't want to consider having a baby until you're in your 20s, 30s, or 40s, but your body gets ready ahead of time (just 100 years ago, it was common for girls to start having babies and families in their teens—that's what people did back then). In order for an egg to be fertilized by sperm and develop into a baby, eggs have to be released from your ovaries. This is called ovulation. You're born with all your eggs sitting there in your ovaries, where they remain until puberty. Then, once a month (about every 28 days), an egg is released. The egg travels down the **fallopian tube** and into your **uterus**, where it remains for a day or two. If it isn't fertilized by sperm, it flows out of your body through your vagina. These eggs are tiny, so you're unlikely to ever see one when this happens.

So what is all of the blood associated with getting your period? A blood-like substance lines your uterus (the **uterine lining**) in preparation for the possibility of a fertilized egg growing into a baby. If the egg is fertilized, this lining offers it protection and **nourishment**. However, if an egg is left unfertilized, this blood-like lining is not needed. Your uterus sheds this lining, and the lining plus the egg flow out through your vagina.

When you first get your period, you may notice that the blood is not quite red, but more of a brownish color. You may see little spots of brown or red on your underwear (sometimes called spotting). During the first year or two of having your period, it's usually not quite "regular." You may experience a lot of blood flow on some days and not others. You may get it every 25 days or every 60 days. This is all totally normal and nothing to be alarmed about. Girls usually settle into a regular pattern after the first year or two of having their period. If you don't, and the unpredictability of getting your period is stressful to you, this is a good thing to talk with your doctor about (either a pediatrician or a **gynecologist**, the type of doctor that takes care of girls' and women's reproductive health). Sometimes medications can be used to help create regular menstrual cycles.

Girls can have very different experiences when it comes to getting their periods. Some may experience cramps in their lower stomach. Some may experience lower back pain. Some may feel tired or cranky, and some may feel full of **energy**. Some will experience a lot of bleeding and some will experience hardly any at all. Your body is different from everyone else's.

All girls can benefit by being prepared for their first period. You don't want blood to stain your underwear and clothes. There are a growing number of options for how to handle these practical issues that come with getting a period. It may be easiest when you first get your period to use a **pad** that you can stick to your underwear. The bottom side of these pads typically has a sticker-like surface that mostly keeps them from moving around. Once a pad gets moist with blood, you'll want to change it—usually a few times per day.

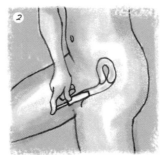

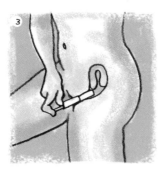

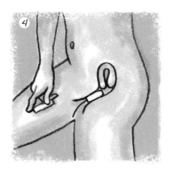

Another option is to use a **tampon**. Tampons are almost like a (small) stopper or plug that you'd use to keep the water from going down the drain in a bathtub, but they're made of a substance that resembles the top of a Q-tip (aka a cotton bud). A tampon is inserted into your vagina and will absorb the blood while keeping any from leaking out. Girls often find that tampons with plastic applicators are easier to use than tampons without applicators or with paper/cardboard applicators. (The front of any box of tampons will describe which type they are.) These also usually need to be changed a few times a day. Using a tampon for the first time can be a challenge, and you may want advice from someone who uses them. Tampons are generally very safe. This is why many women use them. However, it's important to change tampons regularly. There is a small chance you will develop a bacterial infection (called toxic shock syndrome) if you don't change your tampon regularly.

Period cups

Some girls and women use menstrual/period cups. These may be a bit trickier to use than a pad or a tampon because they need to be sort of folded up and then inserted into your vagina to catch the blood flow. They are removed and emptied a couple of times per day, or as needed. One of the benefits of using a cup is that it can be cleaned and reused day after day and month after month and so has less environmental impact—although menstrual products that are disposable may seem cheaper and easier to use than reusable products, they create a lot of waste that needs to be disposed of. In the long run, they cost more than reusable products as well.

Another option is **period underwear**. These are underwear with built-in padding in the crotch. The advantage of period underwear is that the padding doesn't move around the way a removable pad can. The disadvantage is that, as you can imagine, these underwear need to be cleaned really well between uses. Usually this means rinsing them out in the sink and also washing them in a washing machine. They can also be fairly expensive (US$20 or more per pair).

Q & A:

How do you use tampons and why would you want to?

Some girls have told me that they're afraid to use tampons when they first get their period. It can be embarrassing to try to figure out something so personal, even if you have the advice and support of a good friend or another woman. Most boxes of tampons come with good instructions that include illustrations. The earlier drawing about tampons may also be helpful. Most tampons have an applicator to help you insert the tampon into your vagina. Once a tampon is in place, you won't feel it if it's securely in your vagina. This whole idea may seem strange at first and may require some practice to get right.

A lot of girls and women like tampons better than other options because they're hidden and allow for participation in activities like swimming and gymnastics. Pads can feel bulky and would be seen in most bathing suits (and would absorb a lot of water, making them not really work), but tampons can allow you to sometimes forget you even have your period. However, it's important that you remember to change your tampons at least a few times per day, and more often (every couple of hours) if you have a heavy flow.

Q & A:

Everyone I know has gotten their period. Why haven't I?

Just because you haven't had your period yet doesn't mean there is anything wrong with you. There is a wide age range when girls are likely to get their period, from about 9 to 16 years old. If your mom remembers when she got her period, this can help inform you about when you may get yours. Girls tend to get their period at about the same age their moms did, or a little younger. If you're worried about this, talk to your doctor.

The first time I got my period...

"I was 12 years old, I didn't know what was going on. When I saw blood, I thought I was dying! I told my mom and she cried and brought me a book about puberty. It was fairly upsetting." **Alise**

"I got my period when I was 12. My mom was pretty clueless so my friends and older sister helped me. I actually remember very little about it." **Jenna**

"I was 11 years old, I was at home, and my mom showed me how to use a pad in my underwear. It was sorta unexciting." **Nicole**

"I was 13 years old and at my parents' vacation house. I was absolutely not excited and could not understand why my mom seemed so excited. She asked if she could tell my dad and I said ok. I came out of the bathroom and he said 'I hear you became a woman tonight!' I am still pretty mortified just thinking about that!" **Renee**

Q & A:

What happens if I get my period while I'm at school? Or at sleep away camp? Or, even worse, at my dad's house?

Every girl seems to worry about where they'll be when they first get their period. The problem, of course, is that there's no way to know. People around you understand this. If you're at school or camp, there is most likely a nurse who will be more than happy to help you, and will have pads and other supplies available. All female teachers and counselors have been through what you're going through at some point in their life, so they understand and are happy to help, or to direct you to someone who can, like a nurse.

If your mom and dad live separately, and you're at your dad's house, you can always call your mom or another woman—a step-mom, aunt, grandma, or even a friend's mom—if you need help, or if you just want to talk with someone. You can also try to talk with your dad. He hasn't had the experience of getting a period, but he likely knows something about all of this and might be happy to talk with you. He is probably expecting that this will be happening for you at some point soon, and he may just surprise you by being helpful.

What's normal?

What sometimes gets missed in all the discussions of puberty and the physical changes is that every girl is unique. **No two girls' experiences are exactly the same**. So if you get your period before you notice a growth spurt, that's OK. If you get pimples after you notice a growth spurt, that's OK too. If you're in 8th grade, and you don't notice much about your body that has changed, there's nothing to stress about. It's not uncommon for girls to notice some signs of puberty as early as 8 years of age, and it's also perfectly normal for girls not to have completed puberty until they're 16 years old. Most girls will begin to get their period between 12 and 15 years of age. There are many things that influence when you'll experience puberty, from your **genes** (aka biological factors) to your cultural environment. Your puberty experiences and the timing of all of this is out of your control, but it's important that you understand what to expect, and to be prepared for the changes that you'll experience.

Q & A:

How do you know when you are done? And then what happens?

It's not usually immediately obvious when puberty has come to an end for any one girl. Most girls will finish growing taller fairly early in high school (or even in middle school), but you could be among the minority of girls who grow taller in college. For most girls, getting their period means that puberty is coming to an end and most of the other changes discussed in this chapter — hair growth, breast growth, skin changes — will be underway if not completed at this point. But this does not mean that your body is done changing for the rest of your life. If you are like most people, you may gain weight with age or you may lose weight. Your skin will show signs of aging (for example, you will develop wrinkles and freckles or "sun spots"). Parts of your body may sag or "droop." This is all totally normal, and it is up to you to decide if you want to embrace getting older or resist it.

The number on the scale

It's important for you to know that you will gain weight during puberty and your body shape will change. This is totally normal. Everything about you is getting bigger, even your heart. Plus, you're probably going to be at least a few inches taller at the end of puberty. One estimate is that girls gain an average of 25 pounds during puberty. It's completely normal for your body to have wider hips; this is part of becoming a woman. Some girls like how their bodies change during puberty and some girls don't. Sometimes, your new body just takes a bit of getting used to. If you feel upset about how your body has changed, it's a good idea to talk to someone about this. Talk with your friends, who will be having similar experiences. Talk to your mom or an aunt or another adult that you trust. If you feel like you want to talk with an expert, your doctor, school nurse or counselor, or a therapist can be very helpful.

After high school

For most girls, puberty will be completed during high school, but this doesn't mean that your body stays the same for the rest of your life. There are a variety of things that can affect your hormones, as well as your body in general. Your weight will likely fluctuate from week to week and year to year. There are a lot of reasons for these fluctuations: changes in eating habits, **stress**, the amount you exercise, how much you sleep, changes in hormones, and even just your age (people tend to gain weight with age, even past puberty). Some day you may want to have a baby, and your body will change in dramatic ways again. Changes can sometimes make people anxious, but it's healthy to think of your body's ability to adjust and change in so many ways as pretty amazing

How is this related to body image?

Research shows that most girls' understanding of themselves and their body image develops right around the same time that their bodies are changing due to puberty. These changes are likely to affect body image. Some scientists have suggested that because girls tend to gain weight and "fill out" during puberty (in other words, they're less likely to

be lanky or skinny after puberty), they're also less likely to feel good about their bodies after puberty. It doesn't have to be this way. It's important to realize that changes to your body shape, growing taller, and gaining weight are all a normal part of growing up.

Self-acceptance

I discuss **self-acceptance** a lot more in the next chapter, but it's important to think about it in terms of puberty and the changes that will occur to your body as you age. To some, it feels completely natural to grow bigger and mature, while to others, body changes feel strange and even embarrassing. **Remember that it's completely normal for your body to change as you age.** Even if you aren't sure you like all the changes that have occurred, there's nothing to be **embarrassed** about. There are great books written for girls about puberty that you can find in a library or online. (Be careful not to rely on the internet too much; not all the information online is accurate.) Consult these books if you have further questions, and don't hesitate to talk with a trusted adult like a mother, sister, aunt, cousin, or even your doctor. Everyone goes through puberty eventually, and everyone has some questions about it, so no one will think any less of you for asking.

✓ SUMMING UP #TIMETOGROWUP

✓ Many aspects of your body will change during puberty. Some changes include getting taller, growing stronger bones and lungs, developing breasts, and getting your period.

✓ It's completely normal to experience all the physical changes caused by puberty, but you may not necessarily experience them in the same ways that your friends do, or at the same time.

✓ It's important to focus on accepting the physical changes that take place during puberty and to maintain a positive body image. Reach out to trusted adults for guidance about any of the changes that you need help dealing with.

FIND OUT MORE:

- If you're looking for information about puberty and sexual health that is beyond the scope of this chapter, consider checking out: *It's Perfectly Normal: Changing Bodies, Growing Up, Sex, and Sexual Health*, anniversary new edition (2014) by Robie H. Harris and Michael Emberley. Publisher: Candlewick. I love the scientific detail and honesty in Robie Harris' books about growing up, and you will, too.

- There are a variety of good books available about puberty, including a few in The Care and Keeping of You series. For example, *The Care and Keeping of You: The Body Book for Younger Girls*, revised edition (2012) by Valorie Schaefer (author) and Josee Masse (illustrator). Publisher: American Girl. These books answer many of the questions that you and girls your age typically have about puberty.

- Many books about puberty can be found in your local library, but don't be afraid to ask an adult to purchase these for you. For more scholarly articles and web pages with information about puberty, see the companion website for this book: www.TheBodyImageBookforGirls.com.

CHAPTER 3

LOVE YOUR BODY

#BeYouTiful

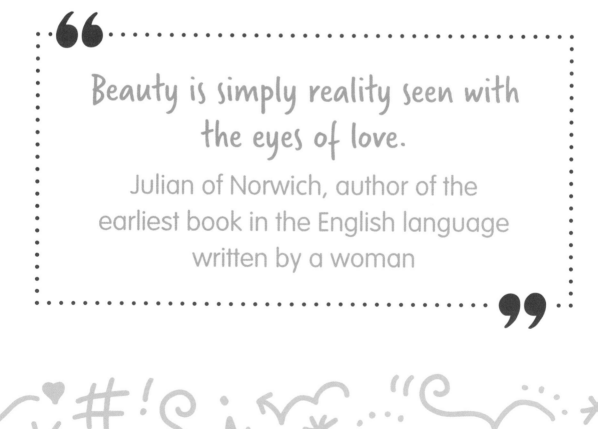

" Beauty is simply reality seen with the eyes of love.

Julian of Norwich, author of the earliest book in the English language written by a woman "

Does anyone truly feel good about their body?

When I was interviewing Shelby (16 years old) in the process of writing this book, she suggested that her body "isn't all that great, but gets the job done." Like her, some people try to be happy with their bodies, even when they're dissatisfied with them. If you look on Instagram or YouTube, it seems like everyone is trying to change their bodies. Most people aren't all that satisfied with what they see when they look in the mirror, at least not after they hit adolescence.

Can you learn to feel good about your body? We don't think much about our bodies when we're young children, but as adolescence approaches, we begin to be critical. We wish our legs were longer or our bottoms bigger (or smaller). We wish for clearer skin and bigger breasts. But why? Long legs, or small bottoms, or clear skin don't make us smarter or nicer people. The desire for these physical features is learned. What has been learned can be unlearned.

IN THIS CHAPTER, YOU'LL LEARN

- some tips to help you stay positive about your body,
- the importance of protecting your body and keeping others from being negative influences on your body image, and
- the difference between adaptive appearance investment and caring too much about your appearance.

There is good scientific evidence that you can improve how you feel about your body. You can even love your body (at least most of the time!). It's not about changing your body so that you look more like Beyoncé or Emma Watson. In an interview in *Seventeen* magazine in 2014, Emma Stone said, "My great hope for us as young women is to start being kinder to ourselves so that we can be kinder to each

other. To stop **shaming** ourselves and other people for things we don't know the full story on—whether someone is too fat, too skinny, too short, too tall, too loud, too quiet, too anything. There's a sense that we're all 'too' something, and we're all not enough."

So how can you start feeling like enough?

Focus on functionality

What is **functionality**? Functionality refers to the ways in which your body moves, works, or functions. Our bodies perform all sorts of functions each and every day. We walk, run, jump, eat, sleep, breathe, dance, sing, swim, climb, and a million other things. Our bodies make all of these things possible.

Scientists who study body image have found that thinking about our bodies' functionality is important. In fact, the more we think about functionality, the less we seem to get hung up on more **superficial** issues of appearance. If you're ever feeling discouraged about your body, it can be helpful to spend a bit of time thinking about the things your body *does*. Start with what you did when you woke up this morning and think about everything you did during your day. Maybe you woke up, showered, got dressed and ready for school, ate breakfast, rode your bike to school, read, wrote, completed a science experiment, talked to your friends, ate lunch, ran during gym class, played the piano, finished your homework, ate dinner, spent time with your family, watched television, and got ready for bed. Your body made all of that possible. That's a lot!

For example, your body digested your food and used that for energy to ride your bike and stay alert at school. Your brain allowed you to do your school work and to have conversations with your friends and family. Coordination between your fingers and your brain allowed you to play the piano. **The human body is truly amazing!**

How do you help your body complete so many amazing tasks? You feed it, you keep it clean by bathing and following other good **hygiene** practices, and you sleep. When you think about it, you don't have to do all that much to end up with a body that can do so many things.

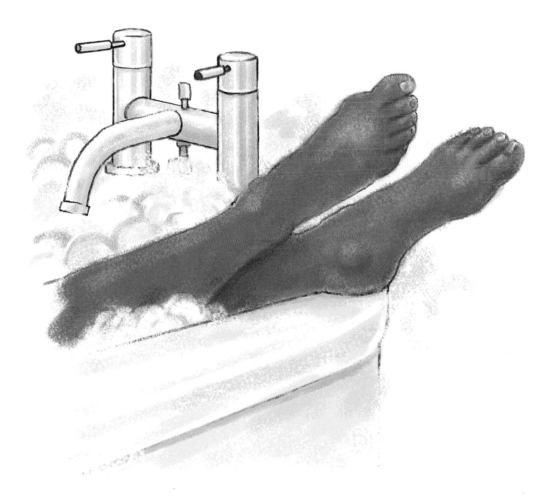

Appreciate your body

Even though your body is amazing, you may be able to come up with things you don't like about it. What things lead you to think negatively about your body? Can you avoid them? For example, if looking on Instagram leads you to feel bad about yourself, you might avoid Instagram, or at the very least, unfollow people who make you feel bad and replace them with body-positive accounts like @healthyisthenewskinny.

One activity that may help you feel better about your body is to make a list of the things that you *like* (or *love*) about your body and appearance.

These can be anything: your eyes, lips, teeth, hair, fingernails, feet, stomach, calves, curves, muscles—anything at all. Add *why* you love these things to your list. Think about this for a few days and try to make the list as long as possible. You don't need to share this with anyone, so you can brag to yourself all you want. Keep your list someplace safe. When you feel down on yourself or upset about some aspect of your appearance, look at your list of the qualities you like about your body. Take a moment to feel grateful for them and try to push whatever negative thoughts you're having out of your mind.

MY STORY

Caren May, 18 years old

Usually I feel fine about my body, but that's not to say that there haven't been challenging moments during my teens. I've been a dancer for as long as I can remember, and dance culture often includes a heavy focus on how your body looks. This was especially true when I was studying ballet. At some point, I became aware that I didn't have a "ballet body," but this hasn't bothered me too much now that I'm studying modern dance more. I find myself feeling more comfortable in my body with modern dance. I still do love ballet, though, despite the toxic environment it can cultivate.

My boyfriend, who is transgender (female to male), has probably been one of the biggest influences on my body image. He obviously has had many issues with his body, and it has made me think more about how I feel about mine. I've come to understand that most of us feel at least a little uncomfortable in our bodies, but that for some people this is truer than for others. Wishing you were a bit thinner is nothing in the scheme of things. Throughout the three years we've been together, we've worked to make each other feel better about ourselves and offer each other support when things feel hard. I've also come to learn that what's healthy for me isn't the same—and doesn't necessarily look the same—as what's healthy for someone else. I think it's really important to understand this and strive for your individual health and wellness.

One thing I wish I had learned sooner is that one of the most essential factors in feeling good about your body is wearing clothes that you like and that you think look good on you. I haven't worn a dress in maybe two years, except for prom and a wedding, and it has really changed the way I feel about myself. You also don't need to be stuck in one style forever. You may feel like wearing a suit one day and a ball gown the next, and if that makes you feel good about yourself, more power to you. Don't be afraid of what other people think. Taking care of yourself—body and mind—matters so much more.

Focusing on appreciating your body and being grateful for aspects of your appearance can improve how you *feel* about your body and appearance. In one of the studies I conducted with some other researchers, we asked people to list only three features they were grateful for about their appearance. Even just making this very short list had a positive impact on people's body image. It's a simple thing to do, but it just may work.

☆ MYTHS AND MISBELIEFS

People will think that you're bragging or full of yourself if you act happy about how your body or some part of how your appearance looks.

Have you ever heard someone say, "I feel soooo fat." Maybe you even responded by saying, "You are not! I am soooo fat!" When people talk like this, **psychologists** call this **fat talk**. Although extremely common, fat talk isn't good for our **mental health**. Talking negatively about our bodies with our family, friends, and even our acquaintances has been shown to make us feel bad about our bodies. The more we do it, the worse we feel.

What could we do instead?

It may be beneficial to be happy—confident, even—about our appearance. The next time someone you know says, "I feel sooo fat," you can respond by saying, "Let's focus on the positive. What are some things you like about your appearance? I like my…" The person you're talking with may be surprised, but also relieved to have a different sort of conversation. They aren't likely to think that you're full of yourself; instead, they're likely to think about their own appearance differently, and more positively. In fact, a recent study showed that the best way to change this sort of "fat talk" is to confront it, not ignore it or join in with it. Changing the direction of your conversation could have real benefits for both you and your friend.

Self-compassion

Sometimes many of us think about and treat ourselves worse than we would treat a friend. We may think to ourselves that we're too short or too chubby or not **athletic** enough. We wouldn't tell our friends that we think they're too short or too chubby or not athletic enough. So why do we "talk down" to ourselves like this?

There is evidence that people *think* they benefit from being hard on themselves. They think they'll improve themselves if they **bully** themselves. **However, people tend to benefit from self-compassion**. Self-compassion is basically being kind to yourself and treating yourself like you would treat a friend. Scientists have found that people who are self-compassionate tend to experience success because they don't waste energy getting upset with themselves; instead, they focus this energy toward **motivating** themselves to achieve self-acceptance and success.

The next time you want to tell yourself that you're out of shape or unattractive, take a deep breath. Remember, this isn't a good use of your energy. Think of a close friend. You're as deserving as your friend, so don't say anything to yourself that you wouldn't say to a close friend.

If you're having a hard time feeling accepting of yourself, go back to the lists I suggested that you make earlier in this chapter, and try to focus on your strengths.

Feeling teased—or even harassed

It can be extra hard to appreciate and accept your body if you feel like other people don't appreciate and accept it. In particular, if someone you care about teases you about your appearance, this may lead you to feel terrible. In one study, adult women were asked about being teased about their appearance in their childhood and adolescence. If they were teased, they remembered it! And they remembered who did the teasing (friends and brothers were the biggest **culprits**). The worst part is that these women were also less likely to feel good about their appearance than women who weren't teased.

You can't necessarily stop other people from teasing you, but you can change how you react to this teasing. It's a good idea to tell people if they're upsetting you. Your brother, your friend, or whoever is teasing you may not even mean anything by it; maybe they mean to be funny or affectionate. (People can have a strange way of showing that they care about you.) You can also choose not to **internalize** what they say. Internalizing means taking information that's outside of you and making it your own. If your brother tells you that your nose is too big, you can choose to ignore him or you can make his opinion your own opinion—meaning you start to believe your nose is too big. But you don't have to share his (or anyone else's) opinion about your appearance.

Sometimes people can take teasing too far. Someone may even bully you about your appearance or physical self. If someone says something mean, inappropriate, or sexual about your appearance, it is **harassment**. Sometimes harassment is even **sexual harassment** if it includes things like commenting on your breasts, or it could include touching your body where you don't want to be touched (see the Q&A's on the following pages).

Unfortunately sexual harassment is pretty common, especially of girls and women. Recently, in order to raise awareness of how common sexual harassment is, **activists** and celebrities started the "Me Too Movement" (**#MeToo**). Tarana Burke created the movement and a **non-profit organization** back in

2006, but it caught on in 2017 when celebrities, **bloggers**, and regular people like yourself helped to grow the movement. Celebrities like Alyssa Milano, Lady Gaga, Emma Watson, and Keira Knightley have used social media to start to talk more about their experiences of being harassed. The goal is to make this sort of harassment less common by getting women to speak up when something happens to them, and to keep women from feeling alone if they ever have to deal with harassment.

When a girl or woman experiences harassment, sometimes she is embarrassed to tell anyone what happened. Sometimes she may not even be sure that what she experienced counts as harassment. She may feel angry and upset, but she doesn't always say something to an authority figure. It's important that you speak up if you ever feel harassed. Even if you aren't sure how to describe what happened to you, talk to an adult you trust as soon as possible. It may make sense to talk to the police or even just to a principal or other relevant authority figure. But you don't have to do this on your own. **Be sure to ask a parent or other trusted adult to help you figure out the best way to handle your experience.** And keep in mind that you're doing this for yourself—and to protect other girls and women out there from being mistreated.

Q & A:

What should you do if your friends tease you about your looks?

Being teased about how you look can be incredibly painful—even if the people teasing you love you and are just joking around. A lot of people who develop low self-esteem and eating disorders report that they were once teased about their looks. It's important that you don't let some insulting and hurtful things that other people say rob you of your sense of self. No one looks perfect, and we all have body parts that we don't like completely. It's OK to tell your friends that you find their comments hurtful (or not helpful). If your friends don't listen to you, you may want to talk to an adult about this. It's also valuable to remind yourself that some of our "imperfections" make us unique. They make us who we are and we don't want to totally change them.

Q & A:

What should you do if someone touches you in a way that makes you feel uncomfortable?

It's really important that you know that your body is your own. You should never be touched in a way that makes you uncomfortable (unless it's a medical examination at a doctor's office; sometimes those are not exactly fun). If a boyfriend or significant other touches you somewhere you don't want to be touched, or someplace where it doesn't feel good to you to be touched, it's important that you say something to that person. If a stranger touches you someplace that makes you uncomfortable, it's very important that you say something to that person as well. But you also should talk to someone else about this.

So who can you talk to?

It's a good idea to talk to one of your parents or another trusted adult about what you've experienced. There is no reason to feel responsible or guilty about this. If you don't share what's happened to you, then the person who has mistreated you may go on to mistreat other people as well.

It's OK to care about how you look

Even though you shouldn't let others make you feel bad about your appearance—and you definitely shouldn't put up with any sort of harassment—this doesn't mean that you need to totally ignore how you look. It's completely normal to care about how you look. Did you know that, worldwide, people spend US $382 *billion* each year on perfumes, **cosmetics**, and **toiletries**? Why do people spend so much money on these beauty aids? It seems that spending time and money to make ourselves look and smell nice is important because it reveals to the world that we care about ourselves. In fact, psychologists call this **self-care** (see Chapter 9 for a lot more about self-care). There is absolutely nothing wrong with taking good care of yourself, whether that's taking some time to wash and style your hair, paint your nails, or select clothes that make you feel **fashionable**.

However, if you spend a lot of time looking in the mirror and worrying about your appearance, you may care a bit too much. What's "a lot" of time? It's hard to say, in terms of an exact number of minutes

or hours. It's probably safe to say that you don't need to spend more than about 30 minutes of mirror time to get ready in the morning and maybe a bit of time (minutes, not hours) later in the day if you need to change or get ready to go someplace different. Spending hours on your appearance each day will cut into the time you can spend on homework, friendships, hobbies, and even sleep.

I bet you didn't know that there is even something called the "No Mirror Movement." The **No Mirror Movement** was created by a group of dancers who want to change how girls and women think about their bodies. They teach **mindfulness**, self-care, and body **acceptance** as part of the experience of learning dance. In other words, they focus on body functionality, body appreciation, and self-compassion, which I've discussed earlier in this chapter. It's an interesting way to think about all of this—that we should all feel good in our bodies and worry less about how we look. There are also bloggers who have written about avoiding mirrors and all reflective surfaces for a certain length of time. These individual "no mirror movements" have sometimes gone viral because the bloggers tend to write about how much better they feel when they avoid scrutinizing themselves in mirrors. What if you tried not to look in the mirror for an entire day? Or even half a day? How do you think you'd feel?

Of course, there's a reason we have mirrors in the first place. We want to see how we look—and that's not always a bad thing. When I interviewed Sarah (13 years old) in the process of writing this book, she told me how she always gets food stuck in her new braces. She feels like she's always looking in the mirror and trying to get this food out. I suppose it would be distracting, and even **unhygienic**, if Sarah didn't pay attention to this issue with her teeth. And it would be embarrassing if people were always telling her (or afraid to tell her) about the food stuck in her braces.

MY STORY

Lena May, 21 years old

I feel pretty OK about my body. I like the way I'm shaped, but I used to want longer legs. I felt that my legs and height (or lack of height!) made me look "stubby." I don't really care about that anymore, but I guess that women may often want to look different when trying to fit into certain clothes.

Even though I like the look and shape of my body, I want to tone it up a bit. I'm not in a rush to do that right now. I expect that changing my health habits (diet and exercise) when I'm no longer a student will be easier. I think I'm mostly content with my body because I fit the ideal look for black women, which tends to be that of a curvier body (smaller waist, wider hips).

When I was younger, it was easier to pick apart certain aspects of my body, like my skin tone, nose size, and hair texture. Being a young, impressionable black girl, I wanted the features that were valued in the black community. Ironically, those concerns faded when the biggest preoccupation became my skin. I've had acne and acne scarring for so long, and it has progressively worsened. So all I want is clear skin and I don't care about anything else. It's weird that my issues with my skin made me realize everything else about myself was OK, and not worth fussing over. Unfortunately, I haven't been able to reach self-acceptance with the issues I have with my skin. I think part of this has to do with the fact that acne isn't really focused on in the **body-positive movement**; there's focus on weight, height, disabilities, body hair, and body size and type, but I never see anything about acne. Maybe this is because acne is considered an adolescent issue that you're supposed to outgrow after puberty. But for people who suffer with adult acne, it's easy to feel like the odd one out.

One thing that has really helped me to think more positively about my body image is an online forum that I visit made up mostly of black girls and women. It has been helpful to hear from black women that I can relate to. I enjoy being part of a community that is like-minded, and I think this has helped me improve my self-image in general. My advice for younger girls is to find a community like this—in person or online—that is a positive influence on your body image. There are so many negative influences out there, but there are also positive influences if you look for them.

Looking in the mirror doesn't need to be an opportunity for **self-criticism**. Girls on YouTube may indicate that they spend a lot of time selecting their outfits each day, checking how they look in a mirror, and changing their clothes more than once on some days. You can try to make an effort not to do any of this. Remind yourself that no one else probably notices or cares exactly how your jeans fit you, or which top you wear on any given day. **You can choose to pay less attention to some details of your appearance and focus that time and energy on other aspects of your life.**

Q & A:

I know I shouldn't care too much about how I look, and that there are more important things in life, but I do care about how I look. I think that if I were more attractive, I would worry less. What should I do?

It's hard to not care about how you look. Everyone does, to some extent. And you shouldn't be upset with yourself for caring. You receive all sorts of messages every day saying that it's appropriate—even important—to care about your appearance. Some scientists have even suggested that it's normal for girls and women to think and talk about how they look—that it creates a sort of belonging or bonding among girls and women.

Of course, caring can go too far. There should be other things going on inside your head besides concerns about your appearance. I think the definition of "adaptive appearance investment" is useful for thinking about what is "good" and what is "too far" when it comes to caring about our appearance. Adaptive appearance investment is defined as "regularly engaging in appearance-related self-care, such as grooming behaviors that protect an individual's sense of style and personality; it's enhancing one's natural features via benign (not harmful) methods." According to this definition of what's good or healthy when it comes to caring about our appearance, it's fine to buy clothes that fit us well and flatter us. It's reasonable to take time to style our hair or to use make-up. But it's probably unhealthy or risky to do things that pose some danger to you, like getting a nose job or spending so much time exercising that you don't have time to do other important things (like get enough sleep), or putting your health at risk by following fad diets.

Even scientists who study body image issues admit that it can be hard to know what is "healthy" caring about your appearance and what is "unhealthy." If you feel that you're worried about how much you care about your appearance, try to spend some time on activities that are not appearance focused. Hopefully, some of the ideas in this chapter will be useful. It may also be useful to talk to a counselor about your concerns. The National Eating Disorder Association has a list of counselors on their web page who are trained to help people deal with issues other than eating disorders, including concerns about appearance, weight, and body image. You may want to check that out.

As you grow up, you'll need to figure out what makes sense for you and how much you want to invest in your appearance, in terms of both money and time. But never forget that the people who care about and love you will not think any differently of you if you wear make-up or not, or if you wear nice clothes or just comfy clothes.

Remember: this matters—a lot!

Focusing on the positive and working toward a positive body image is very important. A big part of this is developing healthy habits, such as good eating habits (see Chapter 5 for more about healthy eating). Loving your body isn't just a superficial concern. It isn't just about loving how you look. **Feeling good about your body and taking care of it is important to your health, how you view yourself, and how you view the rest of the world.** It's worth investing some time in yourself and working on learning to love your body if you don't already. You only get one body to last you your entire lifetime. It's important that you're good to yourself!

Q & A:

I look a lot like my older sister, but she seems to get a lot more attention from boys—they think she's prettier. I would like to have a boyfriend too, and I feel bad being jealous of my sister. Help?

It can be very difficult to feel like you're in a sibling's shadow. It's also normal to feel like you want to grow up and do the things that your older sister is doing. Your time will come. Try to enjoy being the age that you are now. Boyfriends (or girlfriends) will come in time.

Most importantly, try to use this situation as practice in not comparing yourself with others. Psychologists refer to this as social comparison, and rarely does anything good come of comparing your appearance with that of others. In fact, research suggests that people tend to feel bad about themselves when they engage in this kind of social comparison.

It's easy to look at someone else's life and feel like it's better than your own, but that's usually because we make social comparisons on just one aspect of life. It may seem like someone else has a better life because she receives more attention from boys. However, maybe she doesn't do as well in school, or isn't as good at sports as you are. Each of us has our own strengths, whether in terms of our ability to make friends, our fashion sense, or our sense of humor. Focus on your strengths and try to be happy for other people when they have success on the basketball court or with a new boyfriend.

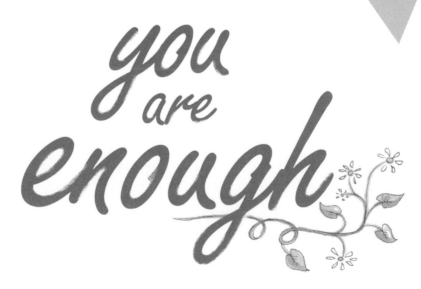

you are enough

✓ SUMMING UP #BEYOUTIFUL

✓ Get into the habit of focusing on the parts of your body that you like and not the parts that you dislike.

✓ Think of the ways your body helps you—dancing, eating, sleeping, and laughing—and always be kind to yourself.

✓ Take good care of yourself and work toward maintaining healthy habits like exercising and eating healthfully.

FIND OUT MORE:

- To learn more about the **No Mirror Movement**, visit their website at https://www.nomirrormovement.org/. Even if you aren't a dancer, and even if you can't attend a workshop, you'll find an interesting perspective to think about.

- If you wonder what it would be like to *not* look at yourself in the mirror, read Autumn Whitefield-Madrano's account of her month-long experience at www.autumnwhitefieldmadrano.com/month-without-mirrors.

- The **National Eating Disorder Association** has a list of counselors on their web page at https://www.nationaleatingdisorders.org/find-treatment/treatment-and-support-groups who are trained to help people cope with eating and body image issues.

- For more scholarly articles and web pages with information about body image, see the companion website to this book: www.TheBodyImageBookforGirls.com.

CHAPTER 4

YOUR IMAGE

#BeYourOwnInfluencer

> "Don't change so people will like you. Be yourself and the right people will love you."
>
> Anonymous

Do you ever watch videos on YouTube? Spend time on Instagram or Snapchat? Maybe you even watch TV shows sometimes? Do you look at magazines? What do you notice about all the girls and women you see on YouTube, Instagram, Snapchat, television, and the other forms of media?

They probably look pretty perfect to you, but there's a good reason for that.

⇨ IN THIS CHAPTER, YOU'LL LEARN

○ how the media is incredibly deceptive in presenting images of ideal beauty that aren't real depictions of actual people,

○ the role that social media may play in your body image and how to become media literate, and

○ the importance of being thoughtful about self-acceptance when making appearance-related choices, from the clothes you select to the cosmetic surgery you might one day desire.

It's just not "real"

Have you ever played with a **filter** on your phone or computer to change how a picture looks? Tweaked a selfie so you look a little better? Maybe you've done this plenty of times. You've cropped a tree out of a picture or made a colored picture black and white. Now, imagine that you could hand your pictures over to a professional photographer. In fact, imagine that the professional photographer took the pictures in the first place and now they are going to edit them for you with all the latest **software**. Your hair will look smoother, your skin will look clearer, and your

eyes will look brighter. Maybe your waist will look smaller, your legs longer, and your breasts bigger.

This is what happens to all the pictures that are posted by celebrities and **influencers** (aka people who have a big following on social media) that you see on Instagram and Snapchat. I've talked with professional photographers in the process of doing my research over many years, and they all tell me the same thing: *everything* is edited. People who are good-looking to start with end up with stunning beauty as a result of computer editing. When you look at famous people online or in magazines or movies, you don't see what they really look like.

Why are all the pictures edited?

Remove blemish

Remove stray hairs

Add highlights to eyes and larger lashes

Cover ear

Fuller lips

Whiten teeth

Red top

Add highlight to nose

The answer is obvious: who doesn't want a pimple **photoshopped** away or a stray hair removed? Unfortunately, the result of all this editing is that girls and women come to believe that there are lots of real people who are physically perfect. This isn't true. Everyone— everyone!—has imperfections.

Movies and videos are edited and staged, as well. There's lighting, filters (yup, for video, too), and professional make-up artists. There are **stylists** and editors who can do all sorts of things to change the way a person looks.

Off-screen, celebrities and influencers are able to change their appearance using other means such as **cosmetic surgery** (and other **enhancements** like Botox (Botulinum toxin), veneers, or permanent tattooing of eyebrows; more on all of that later in this chapter). The main point is this: What you see is *not reality*. Because these images aren't accurate, you shouldn't compare yourself with them.

The images you see are **manipulated** for another reason, too. They're usually intended to sell you a product or a service. Sometimes you're being sold the idea that perfect beauty is possible. Celebrities and influencers appear on social media looking perfect to sell everything from make-up to clothes to household goods. That skin cream that you think you *need now*—where did you first see it? Was it an ad on YouTube? An Instagram post by an influencer? It's all advertising and you probably don't *need* it.

But you're smart enough not to be fooled, right?

We like to think that we're unaffected by advertising. Because we know that people are trying to sell us products, we believe we can escape the influence. The problem, though, is that you see so very many **advertisements** each day, in so many different forms of media, that it's virtually impossible to tune them all out.

Researchers who study how media contributes to body image have found, across many different studies, that **media *does* affect body image**. The media presents an **unrealistic** ideal of beauty that affects us all. In particular, seeing "perfected" and photoshopped images of girls' and women's bodies has a negative impact on girls' (and women's) feelings about their bodies, and their feelings in general. What this means is that looking at these

sorts of images tends to make girls think, "I wish I looked like that" and "I don't like how I look, because I'd rather look like that." Girls also may feel sad or anxious as a result of seeing these images.

A big part of the reason girls often feel bad when they view models on Instagram, or movie stars in videos, is due to **social comparison**, a concept first described in Chapter 3. Part of growing up is figuring out who you are and who you want to become. It's hard to sort these things out. You could ask your mom for help in figuring out who you are, but she may tell you that you're "nice" and "pretty."

The problem is that you know she's probably a bit **biased**, because she's your mom. You could ask a friend how she views you, and she may tell you that you're "fun" and "talkative." She's probably biased, too. Most people who know you may offer only biased, positive feedback about who you are. People who don't really know you can't help with this dilemma. You're likely to look at other people when trying to figure out who you are and who you want to be. You may decide that you want to have a haircut like the singer Lorde, and be bold and funny like the rapper Cupcakke. Maybe you want to buy clothes like a popular girl at school, or you want to be athletic like your older sister.

MY STORY

Daisy Rose, 16 years old

I feel comfortable in my body at some moments and uncomfortable in others. In a world of Photoshop and supermodels, it's very easy to get lost in impossible standards of beauty. As a teenage girl, it's hard to tell yourself that these photos are all fake when your feelings tell you that this is what you should look like.

I have learned that these insecurities are normal, though. And I am trying to learn to appreciate what my body can do for me. I've been a swimmer most of my life and I know that I need food to energize my workouts. My size (I'm 5' 10") is advantageous to a swimmer.

My message for younger girls is to appreciate the fact that you can do what you do with the body you were given. Also, learn to appreciate and recognize the beauty of your body and others' bodies. Don't wish for the body they have, but compliment them and compliment yourself as well. Speaking of compliments, if someone compliments you, take the compliment—it's OK for others to think positively about you and to feel good about yourself.

In the process of thinking about your own identity, you look around at others and compare yourself with them. This is what social comparison is, and it's a valuable way to acquire information about yourself. Obviously, it matters a lot who you compare yourself with. If you want to do well as a student, it may be a good idea to compare your study habits with those of your successful classmates. Comparing your practice habits with those of the team captain may help you become better at field hockey. But you probably shouldn't compare yourself with celebrities. I've already noted that it's impossible to know what they really look like, because the images you see of them are edited. Celebrities are likely older than you, too, and have more money to spend on their appearance. They have expensive hair stylists, photographers, photo editors, and even people who help manage their image using social media (in other words, the posts they put on Instagram are often due to someone else posting for them). In addition to issues of **presentation**, famous people and influencers are unlikely to be like you in a whole bunch of other ways.

Just be you

There's a good chance that if someone has become famous, they weren't all that average to start with. This may sound depressing—it's not meant to—but you're probably average. Because that's the definition of average! "Average" is the way we describe what most people are like. There is nothing wrong with being average. In fact, if you think about it, there's something freeing about accepting that you're a normal, average person. Sure, you're special in many ways that the people who care about you appreciate. But you don't have to be exceptional or especially unique, or strive for fame. You can just be you.

Instead of growing up comparing yourself with a model or superstar, maybe it makes sense to recognize that that's not who you are. It may even be valuable to appreciate what the average woman looks like. The average woman in the USA is 5' 4" (162 cm) tall and weighs about 166 pounds (75 **kilograms** or kg). In the UK, the average woman is 5' 5" (165 cm) tall and weighs about 154 pounds (70 kg). However, the average female *model* is 5' 7" (170 cm) tall and weighs 114 pounds (52 kg). This means that the typical model you see online or in magazines has an unhealthy weight, according to the **Centers for Disease Control and Prevention (CDC)**. In contrast, the average woman is considered **overweight**, according to the CDC.

Where does that leave you? First of all, remember that the models you see may not only have make-up and filters making them look the way they do, they also have body **proportions** that you're very unlikely to ever have. Models are a small minority of all people who are likely to be naturally tall and lean, and they're also likely to not eat enough to maintain good health. I'm not suggesting that you aim to be overweight, but I want you to appreciate that many, many more women in real life look at least somewhat overweight rather than like the women you may be tempted to try to look like. Let that sink in.

"Liking," "friends," and "followers"

Even if you do your best to ignore celebrity culture all together, you'll still be affected by the other people around you. In fact, with **social media** (such as Instagram, Snapchat, and Twitter) use on the rise, alongside people from your school and community you may be virtually connected with a large **social circle** of people you don't really "know."

A recent study of more than 1,000 teens (aged 13–17 years) in the USA found that 70% use social media multiple times per day. Most teens report liking social media, which makes sense—otherwise you'd have to wonder why so many of them were using it! Where results from this study get a bit more interesting is in the questions about **self-presentation** (how teens try to present themselves on social media) and well-being. A lot of teens say that they present themselves how they actually are. To make matters worse, sometimes teens then "like" their own pictures and posts. But a lot of teens also say that they only share information and pictures that make them appear better than they may actually be. One 16-year-old girl said, "I pretty much just post stuff that makes me look good and makes me look like my ideal self..." Sometimes people refer to this use of social media as posting the **highlight reel** of their lives, similar to how a preview for a movie shows some of the highlights from the movie.

Why is this issue of ideal self-presentation problematic? If teens only see each other's best selves—a filtered, edited collection of the best things they do—it's easy to feel like they don't look as nice as others do and their lives aren't as exciting as other people's are. This has the potential to make teens feel bad about themselves. Here again, social comparison is mostly to blame.

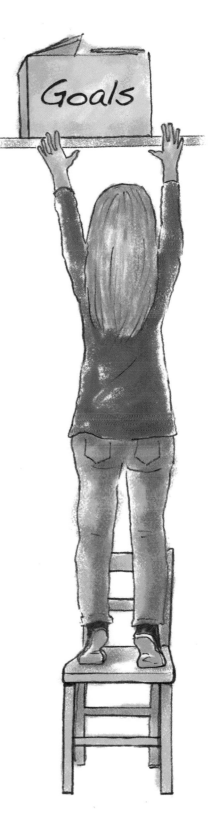

In spite of this, teens tend to report that social media is an important part of their social lives and it helps connect them to other people in ways that they like. This is not all teens' experience of social media, however. Teens who seem to be more **vulnerable** because they don't have as many friends, or because they're anxious or **depressed**, don't always view social media as a positive influence in their lives. For these teens, social media can be a painful reminder that they don't fit in, in a variety of ways, including how they look and their social lives. So one of the important lessons is to take social media with a grain of salt. Don't take it too seriously.

Become media literate

One way to counter the negative effects of social media on your own body image is to become media literate. **Literate** or **literacy** usually means that you can read. When someone has **media literacy**, it means that person can "read" what's going on in some form of media. In other words, they're critical of the media and try to decipher the intention of the media. This may be similar to what you're asked to do in school during reading comprehension exercises that involve reading a passage or story and deciphering what's going on in it.

Why would you need to **analyze** and **evaluate** what's going on in some form of media? As discussed in this chapter, the media isn't always honest in its **portrayal** of people and ideas. Social media may be the worst, as far as this is concerned. To be social media literate, you need to think about people's motivations for posting, the techniques they use to alter their pictures or posts, and how others may be presenting their best selves through their posts.

How do you become media literate?

First, every time you see an image in the media, remind yourself that the image isn't **realistic** and is probably edited and altered in a variety of ways. This is an important step in terms of maintaining a positive body image.

Second, think about why the image is presented the way it is and pay attention to how it makes you feel. Third, stop comparing yourself with images you see and pay attention when images make you feel bad. Replace those bad feelings with positive feelings about yourself and focus on some of your strengths.

BEING SOCIAL MEDIA SAVVY

Because social media doesn't require face-to-face interaction, it's easy for things to become misunderstood and taken the wrong way. Here are some ideas to help you understand and think through online communication, whether it's related to body image or not:

- Just as there are two sides to every story, there are probably two sides to every post and comment. If you aren't sure what someone is trying to say, it may be a good idea to clarify in person if possible. A comment on your new jeans may be nothing but a true compliment.

- Don't respond online when you are upset or angry. Wait until you've calmed down and gotten more information.

- Consider who is posting and what their motive may be. Is a friend trying to make you laugh? Is someone you don't really know trying to be friendly or make you feel insecure?

- Be careful with your use of **sarcasm** and humor. They can be hard to interpret in short social media posts and comments.

- Remember, what is online is almost always still online...somewhere. That includes pictures of you in a bikini on your family vacation. Someday you'll apply for college or a job and you may not want people to see what you've put online. So don't put it there in the first place.

- If it's important to you, deal with it in person. Don't complain about someone you know, fight with a friend, or break up with a girlfriend/boyfriend for the world to see on social media.

Fourth, remember that media is used to sell products and promote the idea that people have perfect lives. No one has a perfect life, and no one needs most of the products advertised.

Fifth, remind yourself that you don't have to engage with any media. And you don't have to be active on all types of social media; you can ease into it, or not use some apps. You can turn off the television, delete an app from your phone, or stop yourself from responding to others' comments on social media. **You have control.**

Research suggests that being media literate can help protect your body image. Girls who are more critical of the media and think about the issues discussed above tend to have more positive feelings about their bodies. It's important that you don't view the media around you without trying to "read" it carefully.

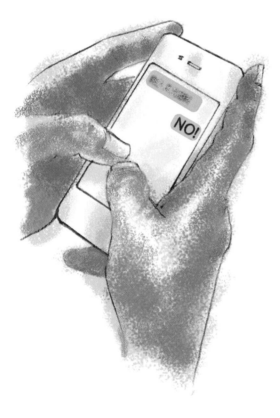

Q & A:

Some of my friends have begun to post revealing pictures of themselves on Instagram and one has even sent a partially naked picture (sext) to her boyfriend. All of this makes me somewhat uncomfortable, but I'm not sure what (if anything) to say to them about this. It just seems like these may not be the best things to do.

Well, your instincts are probably correct that these aren't the safest things for girls to do. It's important to be proud of your body, but this doesn't necessarily mean that you should share it with the world (on Instagram), or even send photos to a boyfriend.

One of the greatest risks is that someone you don't want to see a picture of yourself only partially clothed will see it. Chances are you don't want the principal at your school, a future employer, or your parents to see you partially clothed (in other words, partially naked). Whenever you share a picture of yourself with anyone, you have to consider the possibility that he or she will share it with others or that it will end up archived online pretty much forever. You may adore your boyfriend, but your feelings (and his) could change. Plus, other people may have access to his phone or pictures. So think about your future!

In rare cases, teens have been charged with breaking child pornography laws when they've shared nude or sexually suggestive photos with others. This isn't what child pornography laws were designed for (they're meant to protect children and teens), but they were created before sexting existed. It's unlikely to happen, but because of these laws, it's possible that sexting by those under the age of sexual consent (18 years in the USA) will result in criminal charges.

If you ever feel pressured to send a girlfriend or a boyfriend a picture—or even just a message—that you aren't comfortable sending, stand up for yourself and say no. <u>A person who cares about you will not bully you into doing something that's embarrassing or uncomfortable for you.</u>

If you ever receive a message that you didn't want to receive, such as a picture of someone else partially naked, delete it immediately. You don't want to have "pornography" stored on your phone or computer, as this could also possibly result in criminal charges.

As far as what to say to your friends, if they aren't asking for your advice or aren't close friends, then you may want to keep your thoughts to yourself. But, otherwise, perhaps you can share some of the information above and this will encourage them to change their behaviors.

What not to wear?

As you become a teenager, it's totally normal for you to become more concerned with your image and more interested in what you wear. After all, it's likely that for most of your childhood one of your parents bought your clothes and decided what you wore. It's time for you to take over those responsibilities. Your clothing choices may become an expression of your personality, identity, or preferences. For example, you may want to wear certain brands of clothing, or you may want to wear clothing items that say something on them—anything from your favorite sports team's logo to a favorite band's lyrics. You may enjoy shopping for clothes and selecting items to wear, or you may not. (Not all girls and women enjoy these things, but it's OK if you do.)

You may also sometimes disagree with your parents about what you're allowed to wear. Maybe you want to wear a bikini and your parents want you to wear a one-piece swimsuit. Maybe you want to wear a short skirt and your parents want you to wear a longer skirt. Maybe you want to wear jeans with rips in them and your parents want you to wear unripped jeans. One psychologist has suggested that when parents and their children disagree about clothing choices, it's rarely a disagreement only about clothing. Instead, children are pushing to make their own choices about something and parents are pushing back, not quite ready for their children to have that independence.

Parents may want you to look your age and also to look "**classy** and not **trashy**" (as I sometimes tell my own daughter). Wearing revealing clothes may result in you getting attention from friends or boys, but it may not be good attention. People draw conclusions about other people's personalities based on their clothes. Attention due to revealing clothes may lead others to conclude that you don't have **respect** for your body and that you don't expect others to have respect for your body either. When you're an adult, you can and will make choices about your clothing with less concern about what others think. However, when you're young and going through puberty, you may want to think about other people's perceptions a bit more. You have a lot of your life ahead of you and many important decisions to make about your life. You don't want others to judge you based on what you're wearing and limit your choices, whether it's to get work experience, an internship, or a position on your student council or student government association.

Parents are also likely to want you to wear clothes that are comfortable and functional. In other words, your parents probably want you to wear clothes that do the job that clothes are supposed to do: cover your body comfortably. You may be more interested in fashion and less interested in comfort. Sometimes parents and their daughters also disagree about how much of their body needs to be covered up.

What's going on, and why does it matter how much of your body is covered?

Well, there are a few possibilities. You're probably going through puberty and your body is changing. Your parents may want to protect you from some of the attention that a changing body may attract. Your parents may not be comfortable with you revealing more of yourself than you used to, whether it's wearing a cropped top or short jean shorts. They also may not be as aware of what's fashionable as you are, and they may be paying more attention to what's practical.

Some body image researchers have found that girls' and women's interest in clothes and fashion isn't always about showing off their bodies, but instead about hiding them—more specifically, hiding parts of their bodies that they're not comfortable with. There is nothing wrong with wearing clothes that are comfortable and that you feel make you look your best.

Here's something interesting to think about, though, when it comes to clothing choices. A classic psychology study asked college-aged women to participate in an experiment that involved trying clothes on and then doing activities in those clothes. The researchers told study participants that it was a study about shopping and clothes, but it was really more of a study about body image. Some of the women in the study were asked to try on swimsuits and some were asked to try on sweaters. There was no one else around them to see what they were doing in their "new clothes," and they were then asked to work on a math quiz while they tested the clothing's comfort (or lack of comfort). Guess what? The women wearing the swimsuits did much worse on the quiz. In fact, they got nearly twice as many of the problems wrong as did the girls wearing bulky sweaters. How come? The researchers proposed that clothing that's revealing or less comfortable is also distracting. It's not that wearing a swimsuit decreases your IQ, but most people probably feel more insecure in a swimsuit than they do in loose, comfortable clothes. Wearing revealing clothing may make it more difficult for you to focus on other tasks.

If you feel uncomfortable with what you're wearing, not only may it be more difficult for you to do well on school tasks, but you may also spend time thinking about your appearance in a way that's distracting. Maybe you've found yourself in this situation before? Have you ever worn shoes that are cute but not very comfortable on an outing that requires a lot of walking? Instead of enjoying what you're doing (especially the walking), you may have found yourself thinking that you couldn't wait to go home. In other words, your cute shoes may ruin the outing for you.

What you wear matters for a variety of reasons, not just because of how fashionable others find you. Your clothes can signal to others that you respect and care about your body (or you don't) and that you think that being able to move comfortably is more important than just looking a certain way. There is nothing wrong with caring about your clothes and wanting to be fashionable, but it's valuable to think about what your clothes could say about you to other people. Make choices that make you feel good, not based on your favorite Instagram celebrity's clothing choices.

MY STORY

Lydia Collins, 23 years old

I would say how I feel about my body really changes on a day-to-day basis. Most of the time, I find myself content with the way I look, but I still have feelings that would hold me back from being too showy with the way I dress myself.

When I was growing up, my mom had a strong impact on how I felt about my body. My mom nagged me about not being girly and feminine enough. At the time, I just didn't want to wear dresses because they weren't comfortable. There really wasn't more to it than that. Much later, I started to identify within the LGBTQ community and found that I was attracted to women. Ironically, I also found myself wanting to experiment with dresses and make-up and looking more feminine. It was terribly difficult to feel pulled toward different interests, not sure of whether my family would accept me, and my body image and self-esteem really suffered.

Fortunately, over the last three years, I've come to feel more confidence about my body, which I attribute to my girlfriend. Having someone in your life that genuinely loves and cares for you and supports you helps a lot with learning to be comfortable in your own skin. She has never made me feel that my body image issues are frivolous or unimportant, but she always seems to be able to boost my self-esteem and has contributed to my growing self-acceptance. I've also found myself increasingly resisting societal pressure and stereotypes about gender and sexuality and feeling like I can express myself as both feminine and lesbian.

I think the best advice that I could give to other girls about their bodies is to focus on health and wellness. It's important to take care of your physical health and to make sure that you're nurturing your mental health too. A lot of people don't necessarily feel that they fit into the appearance ideals that society prescribes, but with time you'll figure out who you are and how you want to present yourself to the world. A positive body image comes from the inside, not just how you look on the outside.

Q & A:

A lot of my friends have started to wear make-up to school, but my parents say that I'm not allowed to. How do I get them to change their mind?

If you want to wear make-up or use beauty products, you're not in the minority. One recent report indicated that 80% of girls between the ages of 9 and 11 years use "beauty and personal care products," and 90% of girls between the ages of 9 and 17 use "beauty products." I would recommend talking with your parents about why you're interested in wearing make-up. Is it just because your friends are? It's likely that your parents are concerned about you appearing more grown up than you are, or maybe they even feel sad about you getting older. They may also feel that make-up is unnecessary, both because you're beautiful and don't need to "enhance" that beauty, and because using make-up takes time and money that could be spent in other ways. You may be able to reach a compromise with your parents by suggesting that you purchase some tinted lip balm, or some tinted moisturizer or "BB cream" (a lightweight skin cosmetic that can also moisturize your skin). Maybe you need to ease your parents into the idea of make-up.

A lot of women use make-up, at least sometimes, but this doesn't mean that you should, and it definitely doesn't mean that you ever "need" to. Applying make-up can be fun and creative, but it shouldn't feel necessary. One report found that women spend about 55 minutes each day primping (doing their hair, make-up, and other parts of their beauty routines). That amounts to 14 full days of every year spent on primping. It may be worth thinking about other ways you could spend that time each year.

Accept it? or fix it?

Clothes are one way you may want to try to "fix yourself up." But there are other ways to change your appearance. For example, maybe you're interested in getting your hair cut a particular way, or even changing the color of your hair. Maybe you want to wear make-up, or maybe you even want to permanently change some part of your appearance with surgery.

It's not uncommon for girls and women to think about permanently changing some part of their appearance—their noses, stomachs, or breasts—with surgery. In fact, according to the most recent information available, in 2017 almost 1.8 million surgical cosmetic procedures were performed in the USA. The **International Society of Aesthetic Plastic Surgery** estimates that about 11 million surgical procedures were performed worldwide in 2017. That amounts to a lot of nose jobs, **tummy tucks**, and breast implants.

If you aren't happy with some **aspect** of your appearance, should you consider surgery? Well, there is a lot to say about cosmetic surgery.

First, cosmetic surgeries are very expensive. Some are a few thousand dollars, and most cost much more. According to the **American Society of Plastic Surgeons**, the average cost of a nose job (aka rhinoplasty) is more than US $5,000. Even though most surgeries are safe, there are always risks associated with pursuing surgery; these can range from not liking your new body part to death. With surgery, there is always a slim chance that the medication used to put you to sleep during surgery (called anesthesia), or infections that are a result of surgery, could lead to serious and even deadly consequences.

Perhaps the most confusing issue when it comes to cosmetic surgery is whether or not it's psychologically beneficial. Some body image researchers believe that an important part of developing a positive body image is accepting yourself and avoiding extreme practices such as cosmetic surgery. Furthermore, research suggests that plastic surgery doesn't completely change how people feel about themselves. In other words, if you get a nose job you may like your new nose better than your old nose, but you aren't likely to be happier overall. Your self-esteem is unlikely to be much higher. You're likely to get used to your new nose and not feel like it has changed your life in any significant way once a few months (or years) have passed.

MYTHS AND MISBELIEFS

People who inject botulinum toxin (aka Botox) and dermal fillers into their faces to make themselves look younger are actually injecting poison into their face and may not live as long because of this.

Minimally invasive cosmetic treatments including Botox and dermal fillers have become very popular in recent years. These aren't treatments that you're likely to consider for many years, but it's still valuable to understand them. They work by "freezing" or "relaxing" muscles (in the case of Botox) or by adding volume to the face (in the lips or where wrinkles or indentations have formed, in the case of dermal fillers). All these effects are temporary, usually wearing off within 3–6 months.

In 2017, more than 15 million of these procedures were performed, mostly on women aged 40–54 years old. These products have been tested extensively and have been approved by the **US Food and Drug Administration (USFDA)** for cosmetic use. Like nearly any sort of medical drug or treatment, there can be undesirable consequences to using these products. Side-effects can range from bruising to flu-like symptoms, nausea, and even blindness.

The advice that most body image researchers offer is acceptance. It's good advice, to accept yourself as you are. One important thing to keep in mind is that you'll continue to change physically for most of your adolescence; remember everything discussed in Chapter 2? Even after adolescence, you'll keep changing physically in ways that you can't predict now. **If you ever do decide to make a permanent change to your appearance, wait until after you've finished puberty and you're well on your way into adulthood.**

Love yourself

Botox is made from bacteria that cause **botulism**, which can cause breathing problems, **paralysis**, and even death. However, in the way that Botox is used for cosmetic purposes, these risks are very, very small. These minimally invasive procedures aren't likely to weaken anyone's general health or reduce anyone's lifespan.

There are two other things to consider, however, when it comes to minimally invasive cosmetic procedures. First, some people feel that these have "**unnatural**" results and can make people look "fake" while trying to make them look different or younger. Second, some people feel very strongly that a positive body image means accepting yourself and not taking drastic steps to alter your appearance. Botox and fillers aren't nearly as drastic as surgery, and their effects are temporary. You'll have to decide for yourself what sorts of changes to your appearance—if any—are right for you, and at what point in your life.

Someday you may want to color your hair. Someday you may want to change the shape of your nose. These are personal choices, but make them for the right reason: because you want to do these things for yourself, not because anyone else wants you to. Always consider all the risks and consequences of these choices. Never forget that who you are and your body image aren't just a result of how you look. You're much more than your outward appearance. You have many layers of thoughts, emotions, feelings, hopes, and dreams.

✔ SUMMING UP #BEYOUROWNINFLUENCER

☑ Nearly all the pictures of girls and women in the media are edited, and celebrities have access to make-up artists and stylists. How you see them is not how they look "naturally."

☑ It's normal to compare yourself with others and want to look like people you admire, but try your best to appreciate your own unique qualities and avoid feeling insecure if you don't look like someone else.

☑ It may be tempting to try to change your appearance, whether by wearing certain clothes or having cosmetic surgery, but always keep in mind that how you look is only one part of who you are, and no one looks "perfect."

FIND OUT MORE:

• There is a lot more about teens and social media in Common Sense Media's report, which can be found online: Social media, social life: teens reveal their experiences (2018). Available at: www.commonsensemedia. org/sites/default/files/uploads/research/2018_cs_socialmediasociallife_ fullreport-final-release_2_lowres.pdf

• The American Society of Plastic Surgeons posts yearly reports about the popularity of cosmetic surgery procedures, costs, and other interesting information: "New statistics reveal the shape of plastic surgery" (2018). Available at: www.plasticsurgery.org/news/press-releases/new-statistics-reveal-the-shape-of-plastic-surgery

• For more scholarly articles and web pages with information about body image, see the companion website for this book: www.TheBodyImageBookforGirls.com

CHAPTER 5

NOURISH YOUR BODY

#Nutrition101

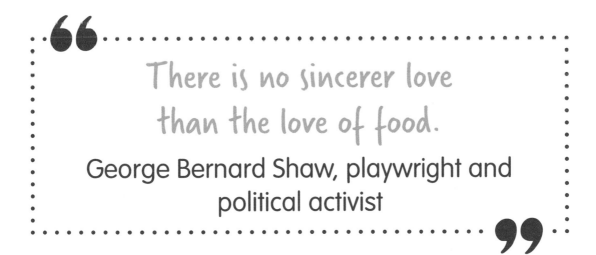

> There is no sincerer love than the love of food.
>
> George Bernard Shaw, playwright and political activist

What and how much you eat affect your health and body image. Girls and women often think about what they're eating and whether they're making healthy choices. Taking care of our bodies means feeding them well.

⇨ IN THIS CHAPTER, YOU'LL LEARN

○ why it's important to eat intuitively and to select healthy foods to eat—most of the time,

○ basic nutritional information about different kinds of food: fat, carbs, sugar, salt, proteins, fiber, fruits and vegetables, and

○ the information you need to think about food as nourishment for your body and healthy eating as contributing to a positive body image.

The "how much" of eating

Once you begin puberty, you may have noticed that on some days you feel really hungry, like a bottomless pit, while on other days you're hardly hungry at all. Believe it or not, this is totally normal. As you go through puberty, you'll grow a *lot* (see Chapter 2 for more information about puberty), and this growth is likely to make you hungry and lead you to eat. Unfortunately, although you'll need to eat more during puberty than you did before, there's no simple way to figure out how much to eat on any given day. One approach to figuring out how much to eat is to pay attention to what your body signals you. You can guide your eating by attending to cues like how full your stomach feels and how much hunger you experience. This is called **intuitive eating**.

We all learn food rules from our culture, like the rules to eat three meals a day, or not to eat before swimming or sleeping. If you're eating intuitively, you ignore most (if not all) of these rules. This doesn't necessarily mean that you just eat whatever you feel like whenever you feel like it. I'm sure you already know that doughnuts every day for breakfast, a burger and fries for every lunch, and spaghetti and meatballs for each dinner wouldn't be the healthiest way to eat. Intuitive eating is thoughtful eating. When you feel hungry, think "What would taste good right now?" and "What would be good for me right now?" Sometimes the answer may be ice cream, but it probably shouldn't be ice cream all the time. The goal with intuitive eating is to pay attention to when your body is full or satisfied, as well as when it's hungry.

We aren't always good at knowing the amount of food we need to eat to feel full. Scientific evidence supports the popular saying that your brain needs time for your stomach to tell it when it's full. Your stomach has to send that information to your brain, and that can take around 20 minutes. This is why after eating a big dinner you may not realize that you're full until you feel uncomfortable 20–30 minutes later. You didn't feel that full while you were eating your third piece of pizza, but once your brain caught up with what was going on, you started to realize that you'd feel better if you undid that top button on your jeans.

Paying attention to your body and your habits is really important. **You want to feel nourished by food, to enjoy eating, and to create healthy habits that you'll stick with as you become an adult.**

The "what" of eating

What should you eat? The simple answer to this question is: **Anything and nearly everything—in moderation.** Some foods are much better for your body than others, but this doesn't mean that you need to completely avoid unhealthy options. As you've probably figured out by now, sometimes the unhealthy foods—sweets, cake, chips, crisps, or ice cream—taste good! The next chapter will discuss in more detail why it can actually be valuable to eat some of these foods even though they aren't super healthy. The main point I want to make for now is that you don't need to totally give up any food that you enjoy. But you do want to be sure that you're eating enough foods that are nutritionally valuable so that you continue to grow and protect your health.

How exactly is the **nutritional value** of food measured? There are a variety of ways that foods can be categorized. What I mean by nutritional value is that foods provide various types of nutrition—through **proteins, carbohydrates, fats, vitamins,** and **minerals**—and these have an impact on our health. Throughout this chapter, I describe these different types of nutrition so that you can be an educated eater, not because you should eliminate particular foods from your diet, and **not because you should feel guilty about what you eat.**

Food's "energy value"

Food is often described by how many calories it contains. A **calorie** is a unit of measurement that indicates the energy potential of a substance (it is also often written as **kilocalorie** or **kcal**). How much energy you need to get from your food depends on a lot of factors. Bigger people need more calories to keep their bodies running well. It's like when you heat a house: a bigger house will need more heat than a smaller house to keep it just as warm. If you're a very **active** person, you'll also need more calories to keep your body working because you burn energy or calories when you exercise. Boys and men also tend to need more calories than girls and women. However, focusing on specific calorie information is probably less important than focusing on eating healthy foods and listening to your body's signals of hunger and fullness. So, what are healthy choices and what aren't? The rest of the chapter provides an overview of some of the specifics.

Fat

Perhaps no nutrient is more confusing these days than **fat**. You've probably heard of fat as being mostly bad for you. Or maybe you've heard of **ketogenic diets**, which suggest that it's healthiest to get most of your energy from fat. In other words, people who recommend ketogenic diets are saying that fat is good. If you're like most people, you may have no idea what to think about fat—how much to eat it or how much to avoid it.

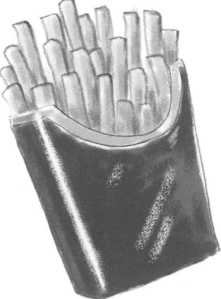

Here is what nutrition scientists currently know when it comes to fat. Without any doubt, fat is more calorie-dense than any other food nutrients, such as protein.

If you eat just a little bit of something high in fat, like a small cookie, it will likely be high in calories. With that **density** comes a feeling of fullness, so if you eat something high in fat you're likely to feel full faster and longer than if you eat something that's low in fat. This can be good, especially if you know that you won't be able to eat again for many hours.

But if you're going to eat every few hours, or whenever you're hungry, do you need to consume fat? The answer is "yes," but it depends on what kind of fat you eat. There are actually different kinds of fat; for example, you may have heard that nuts contain "good fat" (**unsaturated fat**). Foods that contain unsaturated fats, such as nuts and avocados, don't have the same effect on your health as **saturated fats**. In contrast, saturated fats raise your **blood cholesterol**; these include foods such as butter, cream, cheese, and most meat. Limiting your intake of foods high in saturated fats can lower your blood cholesterol, which will lower your risk of some health problems later in life, including **heart disease** and some **cancers**.

The **bottom line** is that it's perfectly fine to consume foods containing fat, but it's best to try mostly eating foods that contain unsaturated fats. "Natural" foods (such as salmon, olives, and avocados) are likely to contain unsaturated fats, in contrast to processed foods (such as store-bought sweets or pizza), which are likely to contain saturated fats.

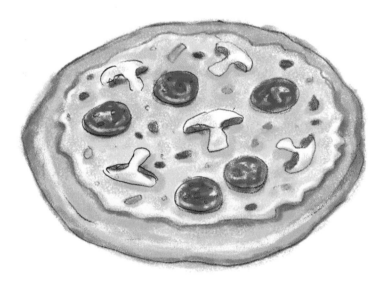

Carbohydrates

Carbohydrates (aka "**carbs**") tend to get a bad rap. In fact, some diets (for example, the **Atkins** and **paleo diets**) focus on reducing carbs in order to lose weight. However, it's nearly impossible to completely eliminate carbs from your diet and you shouldn't try to.

Carbohydrates are an important part of your daily food intake for many reasons. Perhaps most importantly, carbs are an easy, fast source of energy for your body. This is partially why you may have heard of athletes "**carb loading**," or eating a lot of pasta before an athletic event. Having a lot of carbs in your system ready for use may improve athletic performance (although there are a lot of other things that affect athletic performance). Carbs are often tasty—think of warm, fresh bread—and fill you up quickly.

Like fats, not all carbs are alike, and some are better for you than others. Plain white bread doesn't have much nutritional value and may contain processed ingredients that aren't especially healthy. Doughnuts are delicious but are typically fried in oil, making them high in saturated (unhealthy) fat. So what carbs are best to eat?

Smart carbohydrate options include brown rice, oatmeal, and multigrain bread. Many fruits and vegetables (for example, apples and spinach) are also high in good carbs and are a good source of other nutrients as well. Healthy carbohydrates have been found to help promote heart health.

The **bottom line** is that carbohydrates are a great source of energy for our bodies. According to the **Mayo Clinic**, a respected medical institution in the USA, nearly half of your diet should be made up of carbs. It's healthiest, however, to eat mostly whole grains and healthy, unprocessed types of carbs.

Q & A:

My mom always seems to be on some low-carb approach to eating and has been talking a lot about "good carbs" and "bad carbs" lately. What's the big deal? Is there something wrong with eating carbs?

The easy answer is no, there is nothing wrong with eating carbs.

However, it's not just your mom who may be choosing to cut down on the carbs she eats. A lot of popular diets in recent years focus on cutting back on carbohydrates—especially processed carbohydrates. Why? Believe it or not, there isn't a clear, scientific reason to avoid carbs, but numerous diet plans suggest they should be avoided. It's actually quite confusing.

Avoiding carbs may be popular advice because there are so many types of carbs that aren't all that healthy—white bread and pasta, chips, and packaged sweets, for example. These foods taste good, are easily overeaten, tend to be heavily processed, and contain relatively few nutrients. It's not a bad thing to (mostly) cut them out of your diet.

Carbohydrates also cause you to retain fluids, so when people stop eating them they may lose some weight quickly. This isn't to say that people will keep that weight off. (More on that in the next chapter.)

So don't be afraid to eat carbs! It doesn't hurt to try to make mostly healthy carb choices.

Salt

Salt may be one of the most misunderstood substances in our diet. Salt is made up of the chemical compounds sodium and chloride, which are both essential to human survival. And yet you've probably heard people around you mention their desire to reduce their salt intake.

Salt (aka sodium, when it comes to food labels) helps to preserve (or keep from going bad) many foods we consume and makes most foods taste better, so it's everywhere. Even food that doesn't taste salty often has salt in it, including most bread, pizzas, and sandwiches. If you look through the fridge and cabinets in your house and read some food labels, you may be surprised. You'll find some of what I did: one can of black beans = 120 milligrams (mg) of sodium, one piece of bread = 210 mg of sodium, one serving of mozzarella cheese = 170 mg of sodium, and one serving of chicken noodle soup = 700 mg of sodium. You can see how this adds up pretty fast.

Is there anything wrong with salt? Salt can contribute to **water retention** and **constipation**. More importantly, it has been associated with high blood pressure and heart disease. Because of this, the American Heart Association recommends that all of us keep our salt intake to around 1,500 mg a day. Most people consume 3,400 mg daily. One teaspoon of salt is approximately 2,300 mg of sodium.

Some doctors have recently found that the link between salt and heart health has been overstated. In fact, there may not be a lot of evidence to support switching to a low-salt diet. Or, because **potassium** helps rid your body of sodium, it may be better to increase your potassium intake. So what should you do? Probably nothing. Unless you know that high blood pressure and heart problems run in your family—in which case it makes sense to be as cautious as you can be—you probably don't need to worry that much about your salt intake.

The **bottom line** is that salt makes food taste better and last longer, but it may be associated with high blood pressure and poor heart health when eaten in high amounts. Because scientists and doctors still don't fully understand the links between salt intake and health, the best thing to do may be to follow general health recommendations and try to include as many unprocessed, unpackaged foods in your diet as possible.

Sugar

Did you know that the average American eats 22 teaspoons of **sugar** per day? Like salt, sugar has a way of sneaking into foods you wouldn't expect. Bread, chicken nuggets, granola bars, and yogurt (and even ketchup) are all surprisingly high in sugar. You may not realize that sugar is in a lot of these products because sugar is often called other things: **high-fructose corn syrup**, cane sugar, **dextrose**, fruit **juice concentrate**, or one of dozens of other names.

Most of the sugar we consume doesn't come right out of a container of sugar, but is found in processed foods. **Soda**, juice, and some breakfast cereals are among the biggest culprits. Sugar is in so many foods because it often makes them taste better. And as we all get used to eating packaged foods with a lot of sugar added, we seem to crave sugar more and more.

What's the problem with eating sugar? Sugar consumption has been linked to rising obesity rates in the last few decades, which isn't to say that eating some sugar and sugary foods is a problem. The biggest concern may be that eating processed,

sugary foods is likely to take the place of healthier options. For example, a bowl of berries would be a **nutritious** and healthy dessert, but most of us would prefer to have those berries in a pie or on top of vanilla ice cream. The pie and ice cream would probably mean we'd eat fewer berries and we'd eat more saturated fat (in the ice cream and pie crust).

The **bottom line** is that it would be difficult to avoid all sugar and it isn't necessary to do so. It's a good idea, however, for the sake of your health, to try to avoid processed, sugary foods and to stick to healthier options like fruits and vegetables, which I'll discuss next.

Fruits and vegetables

I'm sure you've heard that fruits and vegetables are good for you, but I bet you don't eat enough of them. Most people don't, but we all should. In fact, it's nearly impossible to eat too many fruits and vegetables because they're such a good source of all kinds of nutrients.

The US Department of Agriculture recommends that half of each meal and snacks be made up of fruits and/or vegetables. Half! While this may not seem realistic—a lot of us probably don't have time in the morning to eat a lot of fruit, and vegetables probably don't seem appetizing at 7 am—fruits and veggies should be a big part of our daily diet.

Why are fruits and vegetables this important? They contain important nutrients including **folate**, **magnesium**, potassium, **fiber**, vitamin A, vitamin C, and vitamin K. They also don't have a lot of the bad stuff in them, such as **preservatives**, additives, and salt and sugars that come with store-bought and packaged foods. It's also important to remember that fruits and vegetables can be delicious. You may want to explore new varieties and new ways of finding them, such as dried, frozen, or canned (more on that below), and different ways of preparing them (roasting and stir frying, for example).

The **bottom line** is that fruits and vegetables are an important part of a healthy diet. Try to eat at least some sort of fruit and vegetable each day, and ideally at most meals.

Proteins

Proteins are an important part of a balanced, healthy diet. Proteins help your bones, muscles, cartilage (soft, connective tissue found in the body), and skin to grow. They're also important for hormone functioning. Foods that are high in proteins make you feel full more quickly than foods that are lower

⭐ MYTHS AND MISBELIEFS

Instead of eating fruit, it's just as healthy to drink fruit juice.

In recent years, juicing has become popular. This is just another way of saying "drinking juice" instead of eating solid foods. "Juicing" also refers to blending up fruits and veggies in a blender and drinking them.

It's true that drinking nutrients can be faster and easier than eating them. If you're blending up fruits and veggies at home, this may be a great way to drink nutrients. However, most store-bought juice isn't as healthy as the fruit (or vegetable) it comes from. For one thing, most juice contains added sugars to make it taste sweeter. Although there is nothing wrong with consuming some sugar (see the section above about sugar), it's healthier to eat the whole fruit without the sugar. Sometimes a lot of sugar is added to juice. In fact, some juices contain relatively little in the way of fruits or vegetables and as much sugar as a soda. In these cases, actual fruits and vegetables are much healthier than juice. Fruits and vegetables also typically contain some fiber, which is extracted when juice is made. Fiber has health benefits that make solid fruits and vegetables a better choice than juice.

In summary, it's not true that drinking juice is typically as healthy as eating fruits or vegetables, and it may be worth checking the labels of the juices that you may want to drink regularly. Juice can be a healthy option, if you make good choices that don't contain a lot of sugar or other additives and preservatives.

in proteins. Eating proteins is likely to keep you from feeling hungry. And the good thing is that, unlike some of the other nutrients discussed in this chapter, it's usually pretty easy to get the daily recommended amount of proteins. According to the US Department of Agriculture, most people eat enough proteins without trying to.

If you're looking to improve your healthy food choices, think about adding healthy proteins into your daily habits. Although most of us are likely to get proteins from meats like beef and chicken, other kinds of proteins are somewhat healthier. Beans, peas, soy products (for example, tofu), nuts, and seeds are all excellent choices. Seafood such as salmon can also be a healthy way to increase the protein in your diet.

Q & A:

Is it healthy to drink milk? Does it matter which kind you drink?

The short answers to these questions are "yes" and "yes." Most nutritionists recommend that people drink water and milk, and hardly anything else. Most other drinks tend to be high in sugar or other ingredients that are relatively unhealthy. Milk is a good source of protein and calcium, both of which are important to your body as you grow. Most milk is also high in potassium, vitamin A, and vitamin D. All of these nutrients can be hard to find in other foods, so it's wonderful if you can drink them in milk.

There are many different varieties of milk. They vary mostly in terms of the percentage of fat included, from nonfat to full fat (3–4% fat) milk. The benefits of drinking milk outweigh any concerns about the fat content. Some people are lactose intolerant, or may get an upset stomach when they drink milk. This condition is similar, although not exactly the same, as a food allergy. If you're one of these people, you may want to try lactose-free milk, or nondairy milks like almond milk, soy milk, coconut milk, and oat milk. Most of these have nutritional benefits similar to regular milk, but you may want to check the nutrition label to be sure. If you don't particularly like milk, you may like chocolate milk. There are other sorts of flavored milks as well. The downside of drinking flavored or sweetened milk is that they tend to be relatively high in sugar. But even chocolate milk or hot chocolate still contains a great deal of nutritional value, making it a good snack or treat.

The **bottom line** is that proteins are an important part of a healthy diet, but you're likely already eating plenty of proteins. You may think about trying some new and different kinds of "lean proteins" that come from vegetables and other plants, and keeping the majority of your meat proteins to healthy varieties like chicken.

Fiber

Maybe you've heard the word **fiber** but don't know exactly what it is. Fiber is food that isn't digested or absorbed by the body. That probably sounds weird, but there are actually (parts of) foods that pass through your body without really changing much. These foods tend to be bulky, filling, and come from natural (not processed) sources. Foods that are high in fiber include apples, artichokes, barley, beans, Brussels sprouts, carrots, citrus fruits, nuts, oats, peas, prunes, raspberries, wheat bran, and whole-wheat flour.

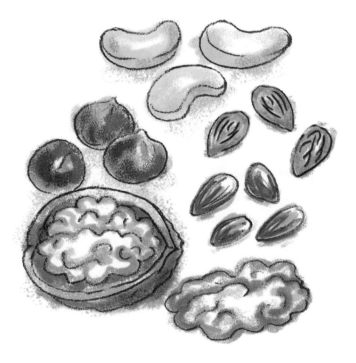

There are many benefits to eating foods high in fiber, including healthy digestion, a lowered risk of **diabetes**, better heart health, lowered cholesterol, healthy blood sugar levels, and regular bowel movements (better than the alternative—constipation!).

The **bottom line** is that including foods high in fiber in your regular eating habits is good for your health. Foods that contain a lot of fiber, such as most fruits and vegetables, tend to be good for your health in a variety of other ways, too.

Q & A:

Are frozen fruits and vegetables as nutritious as fresh fruits and vegetables?

The process of freezing fruits and vegetables can alter their nutritional value slightly. But as fresh fruits and vegetables "age," their nutritional value also changes. Most research suggests that there isn't a clear difference in the nutritional value of frozen fruits and vegetables versus fresh. Some scientists who study food even suggest that frozen fruits and vegetables are slightly more nutritious than fresh fruits and vegetables.

Because frozen fruits and vegetables are often cheaper and you don't have to worry about them going bad, they can be great to keep in your freezer. Frozen fruits and vegetables can be thrown into smoothies. Frozen peas, corn, and edamame are examples of vegetables that can be microwaved for a snack, or as part of a meal, without much trouble. It's hard for most of us to work in as many fruits and vegetables as we should eat each day, so relying on frozen options is often helpful.

Vitamins and minerals

Vitamins and **minerals**—otherwise known as **micronutrients**—are dietary components that your body needs in order to grow, develop, and stay healthy. Some of the most important micronutrients are iron, vitamin A, iodine, and zinc. The catch? These aren't produced in the body, but must be derived from food. Luckily, you don't need them in large quantities.

Most are easily available in foods (and drinks) that you probably eat and drink regularly. For example, most salt has iodine added to it, so you're most likely getting more than enough iodine. Vitamin A is important for your eyesight and immune system, but you're likely getting enough vitamin A in the milk you drink. If you don't drink milk, try kale; it's also full of vitamin A. Iron is important to keep both your brain and your muscles functioning well, and can be found in foods like lentils (and other beans), spinach, quinoa, most meat, tofu, and even dark chocolate. Zinc is good for your immune system and nervous system, and can be found in most meat, vegetables such as spinach, broccoli, and kale, beans and lentils, nuts and seeds, and in whole grains.

The **bottom line** is that if you live in the USA or the UK, the chances are you don't have to worry about your vitamin and mineral consumption. You're likely getting what you need through the foods you eat. If you're concerned, however, you could always ask a parent to purchase a multivitamin for you to take each day.

Some Healthy Foods to Try

There are so many wonderful, healthy foods in the world. Some of them you may never have tried—and you should!

Food	Healthy because...
Almonds	High in fiber, protein, and healthy fats
Artichokes	High in fiber and healthy carbohydrates
Avocado	Healthy fats and carbohydrates
Brussels sprouts	High in vitamin C, vitamin K, and fiber
Cauliflower	High in vitamin C and fiber
Edamame/soybeans	High in protein and fiber
Kale ("baby kale" may be tastier)	High in vitamin A, vitamin C, vitamin K, healthy carbohydrates, fiber, iron, and zinc
Kiwi	High in vitamin C and fiber
Lentils	High in protein, fiber, vitamin B6, thiamin, magnesium, copper, iron, and zinc
Olives	Healthy fat
Quinoa	Healthy carbohydrate, fat, and iron
Salmon	Healthy protein and fat, and high in vitamin B12 and vitamin D
Tofu	Healthy protein, fat, iron

Vegetarianism, veganism, pescatarianism, and other -isms

In the process of writing this book, I interviewed and talked with many girls, one of whom was Gabrielle. When Gabrielle was 13, she decided to become a vegetarian. She realized she couldn't stand the fact that animals were so often mistreated (not to mention killed) when they were raised to become food. She also wanted to adopt a healthier diet. Her dad avoided most meat products for religious reasons and her mom was very health conscious, so they supported her decision and made mostly vegetarian meals at home. Gabrielle has been a vegetarian for two years now and says she feels good about her choice, although she doesn't know if she'll stick with it for the rest of her life.

Maybe you've heard about celebrities such as Beyoncé choosing to be a vegan. People often have very strong feelings about these issues. Most nutritionists would agree that there are pros and cons to avoiding meat and other animal products. I'll briefly describe them here, define some terms, and give you a sense of what the different "isms" are.

Vegetarians typically don't eat meat (for example, beef and pork), poultry (for example, chicken and turkey), or seafood (for example, salmon and shrimp). This may be a healthy—even moral—choice for many people, as eliminating meat, in particular, also eliminates a lot of saturated fat from most diets. There is evidence that the environmental toll of eating meat is much more devastating than most people realize. Some people feel very strongly about not killing animals to provide a source of food for people. However, we also get a lot of nutrients from meat, seafood, and poultry; these foods can be very high in protein and iron (for example, in meat) and healthy fats (for example, in salmon). Human beings have been eating meat products since the beginning of recorded history, and there is likely a good reason for this. It's nutritious, filling, and can taste delicious.

Vegans are vegetarians who avoid *all* animal products. Not only do they not eat meat products, but they typically don't eat milk, cheese, eggs, and other **dairy** products. This means that if you are a vegan you cannot eat some popular foods, such as pizza, hamburgers, and fried chicken. Vegans also may avoid products that come from animals, such as wool, silk, leather, and even honey. For some people, this may be a healthy way to live, assuming they get plenty of nutrients from other foods such as nuts, beans, fruits, and vegetables. However, it can be much more difficult to get the nutrients you need from a vegan diet. It also may be impractical to totally avoid animal products such as woolen sweaters and leather shoes.

MY STORY

Gabrielle Lynn, 15 years old

I've always had a hard time with the idea of eating meat. When I was younger, I'd read a particularly sad story about animal cruelty or see a truck of chickens on the highway and swear off meat altogether. That is, until we had steak for dinner and I forgot all about my prior concerns. About 2 years ago, I heard a podcast on the car radio about how chickens are often mistreated, and remarked, not for the first time, that I wished I was committed enough to actually be a vegetarian. My sister asked, "Well, why don't you?"

After Thanksgiving, my sister and I decided that, together, we would take a stand against animal cruelty once and for all and become vegetarians. While she changed her mind about 10 minutes later, I didn't. I was excited to finally make a difference, albeit a small one.

Since our family keeps kosher and doesn't eat a lot of meat, becoming a vegetarian wasn't a very difficult lifestyle change to begin with. But going out to eat, especially with friends or family, was always a test of my self-control. My sister would have a big plate of the steak I used to love, sitting right next to me with my measly Caesar salad. When we went on a cruise over the summer, there weren't any entrees on the menu I would eat; I had to specifically request a vegetarian alternative from the staff. Although it was difficult, I was incredibly proud of myself for sticking with my decision.

Although my reason for becoming a vegetarian in the first place was simply about the animals, I ended up learning about a lot of other benefits to the choice I made. If more people were vegetarians, this would benefit the environment, reduce pollution, and improve population health. I also began to notice changes that happened in my family. Since my parents didn't want to make food I couldn't eat, the meat consumed in my family greatly decreased. About 6 months ago (after eating a particularly bad hot dog), my younger sister decided to become a pescatarian, too. My family has found meat alternatives, and we've even convinced our extended family to try vegan burgers instead of meat. I know that becoming a vegetarian isn't for everyone, and it has involved sacrifices, but it has also been incredibly rewarding. I love seeing the differences I've created in my family every day.

People sometimes ask if I've lost weight or feel healthier since becoming a vegetarian. I think that I don't feel as much of a physical change as a mental one. I didn't really see a change in the way I look, which doesn't bother me since that had never been something I'd really considered. I think that becoming a vegetarian could be helpful for people trying to improve their body image, but I'm glad that wasn't what I focused on. I'm a lot happier with my diet and my impact on the world around me, which means a lot more to me than the way I look.

Pescatarians are vegetarians who eat seafood. For these people, seafood may be a favored food, or they may believe that the health benefits of eating seafood, and the lower environmental impact of producing seafood, make it a morally acceptable source of food. **Ovo-lacto vegetarians** (aka lacto-ovo vegetarians) are vegetarians who do eat eggs and drink milk. Actually, most vegetarians include eggs and milk in their diets, but sometimes, usually for people of certain religions such as Hinduism, this category is meaningful. **Flexitarians** are "sometimes vegetarians" who eat a mostly vegetarian diet. **Macrobiotic** eaters are vegans who only eat **unprocessed foods** and sometimes fish; they also avoid sugar and refined oils. As with vegetarianism and veganism, these types of eaters tend to want to improve their health and avoid animal suffering and unnecessary environmental damage. However, most of these types of diets require extra work and planning to ensure that you get enough of the nutrients needed, such as protein and iron. Since most people do eat meat, it can be inconvenient and impractical to give up the foods that most people eat. If you're interested in trying a vegetarian (or other "-arian") diet, talk with the people you live with and see how they feel about this, and what they're willing to do to support your diet. Unless you do your own grocery shopping, it may be difficult to make drastic changes to your diet without the support of others, and a lot of parents wouldn't be as supportive as Gabrielle's.

"My Plate"

Hopefully, after reading everything in this chapter, you understand that you can eat anything you want to, but that some foods have more health benefits than others. You also see that the way that different foods (for example, fats) are talked about in public and online isn't always accurate. People can have very strong opinions about food, but this doesn't mean that these opinions are accurate.

The US government has offered a pretty basic way to think about what to eat if you're trying to be healthy. They call this **My Plate** (in contrast to "food pyramids" that kids of past generations were taught about), and there are a few things about it that are worth taking note of. First, the recommendation is for nearly half of each meal to be made up of fruits and vegetables. Second, the recommendation includes carbohydrates that are mostly grains (in other words, "healthy carbs").

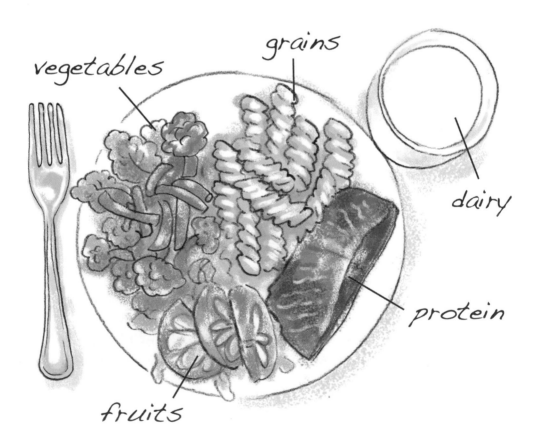

Third, protein is an important component of a healthy meal, but this may or may not be meat; there are many healthy sources of protein, such as beans and nuts.

Most people don't manage to put together each meal to include every healthy option. It's nice to have the goal of eating healthily, but it's a complicated and difficult goal. We'll discuss the importance of thinking about food in a flexible, balanced way in Chapters 6 and 7.

✓ SUMMING UP #NUTRITION101

- ☑ It's important that you listen to your body, eat when you're hungry, and stop when you're full.

- ☑ You can eat all foods in moderation, but do your best to ensure that you eat foods that are especially good for you, including a lot of fruits and vegetables.

- ☑ Eating healthy foods is one important way to care for your body and develop a positive body image.

FIND OUT MORE:

- To learn more about intuitive eating, especially the basic ten principles, you might be interested in exploring the website *Intuitive Eating*, available at: www.intuitiveeating.org/10-principles-of-intuitive-eating/

- The Mayo Clinic's website has scientifically based information about nutrition, such as this page about carbohydrates: How carbs fit into a healthy diet, available at: www.mayoclinic.org/healthy-lifestyle/nutrition-and-healthy-eating/in-depth/carbohydrates/art-20045705/

- To learn more about My Plate, visit www.choosemyplate.gov/

- For more scholarly articles and web pages with information about healthy eating and nutrition, see the companion website for this book: www.TheBodyImageBookforGirls.com.

CHAPTER 6

SMART GIRLS DON'T DIET

#JustSayNotoDiets

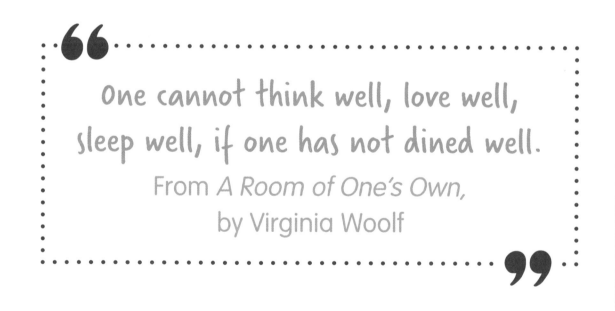

> One cannot think well, love well,
> sleep well, if one has not dined well.
> From *A Room of One's Own*,
> by Virginia Woolf

A few years ago, I published a book called *Smart People Don't Diet: How the Latest Science Can Help You Lose Weight Permanently*. The book wasn't really about weight loss; it was much more about the dangers of dieting. Unfortunately, scientists know more about what does not lead to weight loss than about what does help people lose weight. My goal was to write a book explaining this so people wouldn't do crazy things—that are done surprisingly often—when they want to lose weight.

Most people diet to lose weight at some point. Maybe you've seen this in your home, with your mom, dad, brother, or sister trying some sort of diet. Maybe you've even tried to go on a diet yourself. **Dieting is surprisingly common, which is strange because it doesn't work in the long run.** In this chapter, I'll talk about the problems associated with dieting and present a better way to think about eating. I am not suggesting in any way that you should ever diet. I think it's important to understand the science surrounding dieting so you can make good choices about how you eat and the physical activity that you participate in for the rest of your life.

IN THIS CHAPTER, YOU'LL LEARN

○ how medical professionals measure weight and what is considered a healthy weight for your height and age,
○ why it's so difficult to lose weight, and why diets typically don't work, and
○ how to modify your eating habits to improve your health without dieting or feeling bad about your body.

Your weight is just a number

OK, let's back up a bit. Usually people consider dieting when they weigh more than they want to. This is why it's important to understand what is *healthy* in terms of weight. I'm not talking about what you want to weigh, or what supermodels weigh (many of whom are dangerously **underweight**). It's important to remember that your weight is just a number. It doesn't determine your self-worth, and it doesn't predict everything about your health.

Healthcare professionals make recommendations for weight (keeping in mind your height) that are based on thousands of research studies that suggest certain weight ranges are most associated with health across time. During a visit with a doctor or school nurse, you've likely seen charts that look something like the one on page 97. Your age is found on one edge of the chart, your weight is located on the other, and the **percentile** line where the age and weight lines intersect indicates whether your weight is above or below average for your age. This is one of the most common ways for doctors and other healthcare professionals to keep track of your growth across childhood.

The growth chart in this chapter comes from the **World Health Organization** (WHO) and is meant to present international standards of how healthy children grow. It was developed based on information from many children living in six different countries. Healthcare providers often use these charts as a guide to determine whether their patients are growing as expected. If, for example, a child isn't growing as expected according to these charts, this may mean that the child has a health problem. It also may just mean that the child is petite for her age.

Q & A:

How often should you weigh yourself?

Unless you have a health condition that requires regular monitoring of your weight, then you don't need to weigh yourself very often. Depending on your age and whether or not you've completed puberty, it's normal to gain weight across your childhood and teen years. You're also getting taller and stronger, and gaining weight is a part of that. If you're curious about what you weigh, hopping on the scale once a month is sufficient. At the very most, get on the scales once a week. But don't spend a lot of time thinking about the number that appears on the scales. Your body cannot be measured by just one number.

The weight of the matter

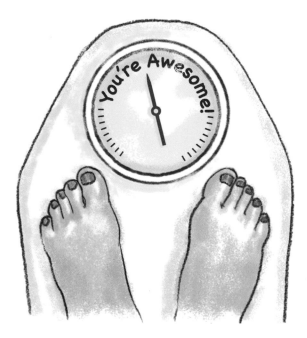

Body mass index (BMI) is a way to measure growth that takes into account both your height and your weight. Obviously, a taller person often weighs more than a shorter person. Most research that examines weight considers BMI, because BMI is a relatively simple way to assess someone's weight status. More detailed ways to assess someone's weight or body composition (i.e., body fat) take much more time, tend to involve expensive equipment, and can be unreliable.

Here is the easiest formula to use to calculate your BMI:

Your weight in pounds ÷ height in inches ÷ height in inches × 703

So, for example, if your weight is 125 pounds (lb) and you are 5' 2" tall (which is 62"), your BMI is:

$$125 ÷ 62 ÷ 62 × 703 = 22.86$$

Another example: if your weight is 90 lb and you are 4' 11" tall (which is 59"), your BMI is:

$$90 ÷ 59 ÷ 59 × 703 = 18.18$$

If you live in a country that uses the metric system, the easiest formula to use to calculate your BMI is:

Your weight in kilograms ÷ (height in meters)^2

If your weight is 57 kg and you are 1.57 m (157 cm), your BMI is:

$$57 ÷ (1.57)^2 =$$

$$57 ÷ 2.46 = 23.17$$

If your weight is 41 kg and you are 1.5 m (150 cm), your BMI is:

$$41 ÷ (1.5)^2 =$$

$$41 ÷ 2.25 = 18.22$$

In order to interpret what your BMI number means, you have to see how it compares with that of other kids who are your age and gender. This is referred to as your **BMI-for-age percentile**. For example, if you're a 12-year-old girl and you are 60" tall (152.4 cm) and weigh 100 lbs (45.5 kg), this puts you in the 68th percentile for girls your age. This means that you weigh the same or more than 68% of girls your age, but less than 32% of girls your age. You're well within what is a healthy weight for your age. According to the Centers for Disease Control and Prevention, being higher than the 5th percentile and lower than the 85th puts you within a healthy range. (If you're below the 5th percentile you *may* be classified as underweight, and if you're above the 85th percentile you *may* be classified as overweight; in either of these cases it may be a good idea to discuss this with a parent, doctor, or registered **dietician**.)

There is another way to figure out your BMI-for-age percentile. The chart below is what medical professionals typically use. To read this chart:

1. Look at the numbers along the very bottom of the chart and find your age.
2. Put your finger on your age, and run your finger up the chart until you reach your BMI (BMI numbers are along the left side.
3. See where your BMI crosses the *curved* line on the chart. These curved lines tell you the percentile of your BMI, showing how your BMI compares with that of other girls your age.

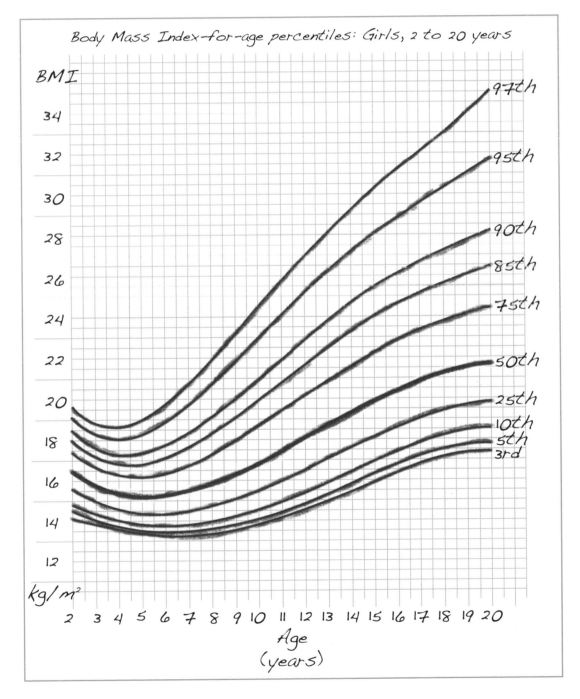

Body Mass Index-for-age percentiles: Girls, 2 to 20 years

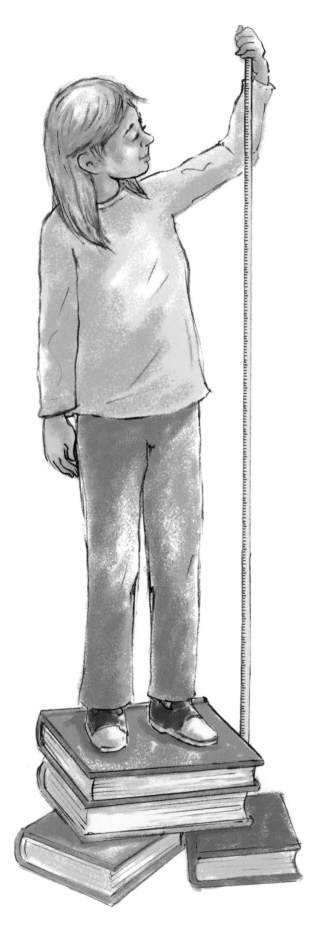

You could also look at the Centers for Disease Control and Prevention's website, which offers an easy calculator to compute your BMI-for-age percentile, available at: www.cdc.gov/healthyweight/bmi/calculator.html

I've included this discussion of weight, height, and BMI and a growth chart in this chapter so you have some of the information that doctors may use to try to assess your weight status, and so you can understand the various charts and graphs you may see. However— and this is *really* important—there are a *lot* of things that contribute to your body size and shape, and some of them aren't within your control. One large scientific study found that the *majority* of both your height and weight may be due to your genes (with environmental factors having more influence over your weight than your height). Scientists estimate that 60–80% of your height is due to your genes. In other words, there's not much you can do to change your height, and there may not be a whole lot that can be done to modify your weight, either. You're however tall you are mostly due to how tall your parents are. Nutrition, medical care, and general health may affect your height a bit, but not a whole lot. Protein is the one nutrient that may affect your height more than any other factor you can change, so if you want to grow taller, be sure to eat protein.

Although weight is *somewhat* more easily changed than height, it's also very much influenced by our genes.

Eating a healthy diet is important for your long-term health, but trying to change your body size or shape by changing what you eat can be very difficult and isn't always a good idea. Recent research suggests that our body size has a lot to do with our appetites, and that our appetites are also determined by genetics. Some people are more likely to feel hungry more often and to have a hard time eating less, if they want to weigh less.

Q & A:

I know that BMI is used as a measure of whether or not a person is overweight, but can't some people be healthy even when they're overweight? Some people are muscular and athletic. People just have different body types, right?

Yes, you're absolutely right. One of the criticisms of using BMI as a measure of weight status (whether or not someone is overweight, underweight or "normal" weight) is that it's just a rough measure and it can't account for people's different body builds. People obviously have very different body shapes. Some women may be heavier, but carry that weight in their breasts, which are made up mostly of fatty tissue. This is often perceived differently from fat on people's thighs or stomachs.

It's important to keep in mind that <u>BMI isn't intended to be a perfect description of every individual's weight.</u> The ranges that have been established for overweight, underweight, and normal weight are based on studies of thousands of people. Scientists and doctors argue that people who fall in the overweight category are at risk of health problems associated with weight, such as type 2 diabetes, heart disease, and some forms of cancer. However, there are many things that contribute to our health aside from our weight. For example, if you exercise and are in good physical shape, you may improve your heart health.

It may seem that all the risks associated with weight—things like heart disease and cancer—will never affect you, or won't for another 50 years. This may be true. However, the eating habits you form when you're young may follow you into your adulthood. It's worth considering the importance of your habits while you're young so you can increase your odds of living a long, healthy life.

Some people don't care as much about food because they don't feel hungry as often. Being hungry is a pretty miserable experience, and it's not a good idea to ignore hunger because you risk not only feeling very cranky, but also not giving your body the nutrients it needs.

☆ MYTHS AND MISBELIEFS

When your doctor tells you that you need to lose weight, you should go on a diet.

Most doctors become doctors because they want to help people achieve good health and recover from illness or injury. They make recommendations that they believe will be helpful. However, most doctors receive very little (if any) training about nutrition, diet, body image, and weight. They can document where you fall on a height–weight chart, but they may not know much about how to educate and support their patients concerning weight. In other words, although a doctor is a good person to turn to with questions about health and well-being, sometimes doctors offer bad advice when it comes to your weight.

If you're ever told by a doctor that you need to lose weight, it's worth getting a second opinion from another medical professional. It may be most useful to talk with an expert who has been trained specifically to help people eat well and maintain a healthy weight. A registered dietician, nutritionist, or even a psychologist with this specialty would be good options for people to consult. If you live near a university, check to see if they have a center or clinic that helps people with healthy weight management. Universities tend to be on top of the latest science, and sometimes even offer free health services to people interested in trying out new medical **regimens**.

Most importantly, if you believe—because a doctor told you so, or your own research leads you to believe this—that you need to lose weight, a diet is not the answer. It may be a good idea to change your regular habits to eat more healthy foods or to be more physically active, but only make changes that you plan to keep for the long term. As I'll explain in more detail below, if you go on a short-term diet of any kind, it's likely to lead to weight gain, not loss, over time. It's also likely to be a miserable experience.

If you weigh more than you want to, then what?

If you weigh more than you want to, or you weigh more than you consider healthy, but you're not supposed to diet, then what are you supposed to do?

It's critically important that you focus on your health and avoid fads when it comes to food.

If you want to change your eating habits to increase how healthily you eat, start by assessing what you usually eat. Sometimes we aren't very good at remembering what we actually eat. Or we just "forget" some of the less healthy foods that we eat. I recommend taking a week and recording everything you eat each day. You can do this at the end of the day on a piece of paper that you keep by your bed, or you can download an app onto your phone or tablet to help with this. When I want to keep track of things like this, I just use the Notes app on my phone since it's with me nearly all the time and it's easy to take notes on it.

After you have spent a week recording what you eat, review your habits honestly. There are likely some easy changes to your diet that would make it a lot healthier. First, look at what you drink. If you drink juice or soda each day, switch to water or seltzer water on most days. This is a good way to cut some added sugars (and calories) out of your diet.

Snack foods are another big culprit in most of our diets. When we're hungry for a snack, we often want to eat something that's tasty and easy to get to. Chips, or crisps, may seem like the perfect snack food, but they offer little nutritional value. We all

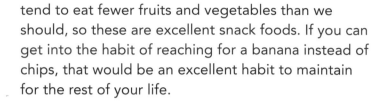

tend to eat fewer fruits and vegetables than we should, so these are excellent snack foods. If you can get into the habit of reaching for a banana instead of chips, that would be an excellent habit to maintain for the rest of your life.

Do you see what I'm suggesting? Basically, make some swaps in your regular eating habits. Take out a few foods that you typically eat or drink that aren't super healthy and swap in some healthier options. Making minor changes to your habits is a good way to improve your health for the long haul. Sometimes it takes days, weeks, or even months to notice that you feel better as a result of eating differently. Be patient! Remember, your primary goal is to improve your health and how you *feel*. Being happy, healthy, and confident is important for the rest of your life, and these factors are all part of maintaining a positive body image. Below I'll explain in more detail why **dieting can be damaging, and a healthy approach to eating is the only way to go.**

Q & A:

My friend's mom is always on Weight Watchers. She constantly talks about the "point value" of all different foods. She says it's not a diet but a lifestyle, and she's lost a lot of weight in the past few months. So, is it a diet? Is it healthy? What are "points"?

Weight Watchers (aka W.W.) typically markets its program as a lifestyle change: a way of eating that you can adopt and maintain for the rest of your life. It offers a lot of healthy recommendations based on good nutritional information. This doesn't mean that this plan is for everyone. Like any lifestyle change, if the recommendations aren't the sort of things you can follow for the long term, they're only likely to lead you to lose weight that you'll gain back again.

Weight Watchers assigns "point values" to foods as a way of helping people make healthy choices most of the time. Weight Watchers helps people determine a certain number of points to eat (and drink) per day, and then people pick foods and drinks that add up to that total number of points. Weight Watchers assigns zero points to almost all fruits and vegetables, which encourages people following the program to eat as many as they want. People who follow this plan can become a bit fanatical as they keep track of and count their points every day, which is why you may have heard of this before.

Does it work? Weight Watchers is likely to work for anyone who sticks with it. In fact, cutting out calories from unhealthy foods in your diet is usually going to lead to weight loss, although it may happen very slowly. Although Weight Watchers isn't a plan I would ever recommend for young girls, it's not necessarily an unhealthy option for people interested in losing weight.

One final thought: you mentioned that your friend's mom is always talking about Weight Watchers and her points. As I mentioned earlier in this book, when we spend time and energy thinking about our bodies and our weight, this is time and energy taken away from other things we could be doing, and we all have only a limited amount of time and energy in each day. It's important that we think about what's most important to us and how we want to spend our time and energy.

MY STORY

Mare Anna, 16 years old

I think I have an average body shape, but when I look in the mirror I see myself as 20 pounds heavier than I am. One of my earliest memories of this was when I was about four or five, and I still had the baby fat that most of us eventually grow out of. I was standing in the bathroom after a bath, wearing a towel like a cape. I remember looking down at my belly and then looking up at my dad and asking, "Daddy, will I be fat forever?"

When I was 12 years old, just starting the process of puberty, my doctor told me I was fat and needed to start dieting. I had a relatively healthy diet at the time, and the only unhealthy thing I did was drink things other than water (occasionally). But I was a determined 12-year-old with a mission to be "beautiful." I made a complex diet plan with lists of things I should not eat. The only thing this accomplished? Making myself feel guilty and worthless.

Now, I currently eat with the mindset of being healthy, listening to my body, and eating things that make me feel energized and happy. I wouldn't say that my relationship with food is what I wish it was, though, and I blame that one doctor for a lot of my anxiety surrounding food.

It probably didn't help that growing up I took dance and gymnastics classes. I would compare myself to the other girls in class and feel awful because I didn't look like them. My younger sister has always been beautiful and skinny, and I always felt that I was compared to her when we were in public. My warped view of my body and constant comparison to others have been unhealthy, but I am trying to accept myself as being beautiful as I am.

So far, my junior year of high school is so much better. I feel like things have really started to change for me. I have a sense of identity and style, and I am beginning to accept myself. The biggest change that happened between this year and last year would have to be the people I hang out with. I now hang out with a group of people who are completely accepting and understanding. They accept me for me. I have never felt closer to other people before and I am definitely happier.

Some lessons I'm learning that I wish I had learned earlier are:

- Strive to be the healthiest you, not the skinniest.
- The only person you should be comparing yourself to is you.
- Do everything possible to eliminate toxic people from your life.
- Your body is always changing, and how you see yourself will, too.

What your metabolism has to do with it

Chances are you've heard people refer to their **metabolism** as "fast" or "slow." People seem to think that having a fast metabolism is a good thing, allowing them to eat more than those with a slow metabolism. There is no easy way, however, for most of us to know with any certainty about the complicated ways in which our bodies function.

It turns out that our metabolism—essentially, the chemical processes that take place within our bodies that keep us alive—doesn't stay the same all the time. The biology that we're born with affects our metabolism, but so do our behaviors. In general, when we eat less food, our metabolism slows down and processes that food more slowly. It's like our bodies want to make good use of the smaller amount of food we're offering them and they use it more slowly. Scientists believe that our bodies work this way because in ancient times it was difficult for people to find enough food to eat. When there was less food around (fewer plants to grow and animals to catch and kill), our metabolism protected us by needing less food.

This isn't to say that we must always eat a lot to keep our metabolism working at full speed—it's not that simple. But we should listen to our bodies and eat what we need to feel full and energetic. If we try to eat too little, our bodies go into a sort of "starvation mode," processing food slowly and often making weight loss less likely. So, as I say throughout this book, there is very good scientific evidence that dieting to lose weight isn't going to work, and one reason is because of how our metabolism works. The best way to keep yourself, and your metabolism, happy is by nourishing yourself properly.

Just don't, just don't, just don't

In spite of everything you've read in this chapter, I know that someday you'll see a **fad** diet and be tempted to try it. Unfortunately, the odds are against all of us avoiding diets, because they're constantly marketed to us. There's always something new, some diet that promises to really work this time. It may seem easy. So you'll think, "What's the harm? Why not give it a try?"

It's possible that you'll be tricked into trying something because it sounds scientific. Or because no one calls it a "diet." It's a "juice cleanse," which is going to make you healthier. Maybe it's a "sugar fast," and you know that sugar isn't particularly healthy. But all of these things are different kinds of diets. **The main reason they won't work is because they aren't sustainable.** You won't want to only drink juice forever, and you won't want to give up sugar forever, so eventually you'll gain back whatever weight you lost trying to "cleanse" or when "fasting."

Instead of falling for the latest fad, it's important to stay strong and focus on your health.

Q & A:

Why is soda so bad for you? Is it OK to drink it sometimes?

You've probably heard a lot about soda being a bad beverage option. There are even taxes on soda in some places (for example, some US cities), which make it cost more and encourage people to drink less (more on that below). But what's all the fuss about? Can you drink soda sometimes?

Soda is often viewed as a problem for a few reasons: people tend to drink a lot of it, it has no nutritional health benefits, and it has a lot of sugar and calories. Furthermore, soda often takes the place of much healthier options like low-fat milk and water.

Diet sodas don't contain any calories, so the concerns regarding soda's effect on weight are less of an issue. But keep in mind that diet sodas contain artificial sweeteners and chemicals that can hardly be called healthy.

Still, it's perfectly fine to drink soda occasionally. It's not a healthy choice to make regularly, but a soda once a week isn't going to hurt you.

So far, research examining soda taxes suggests that these taxes have the desired effect: when soda costs more, people buy less of it and drink less of it. Public health and policy officials often target soda because it has been linked to the rise in obesity rates more than any other single food or beverage in recent years. Again, this doesn't mean that you can never drink soda, but rather that you treat it like a dessert, not something to have every day.

If you have concerns about your weight, and you've checked whether or not your weight is healthy for your height and activity level, talk to a nutritionist, registered dietician, or psychologist. You should get sound medical advice about your weight, and make minor, healthy changes to your habits that you think you can stick with. For example, you could aim to eat an extra serving of fruit and vegetables each day (and maybe drop out sugary cereals, or the chips or crisps you like to snack on). You could get a cookbook and learn to cook some meals that are nutritious and perhaps healthier than what you'd usually eat. Whatever you do, make sure you're focused on your health—how you feel both physically and mentally.

Q & A:

I've heard of the Health at Every Size movement (HAES) and I don't understand how that works. Can you explain HAES?

The Health at Every Size movement (HAES) is an anti-diet, body positivity, diversity acceptance movement. HAES suggests that it's important for people to focus on healthy behaviors, no matter what their size. The idea is to not confuse how people look and their health. In other words, there is so much that contributes to health that you can't just look at someone and decide they are unhealthy.

Nearly everything about the HAES philosophy is consistent with the evidence and ideas presented in this book. Nevertheless, HAES's claim that people who are overweight don't incur health risks because of their size is controversial. There is actually a lot of scientific evidence that links weight and health. In particular, being overweight leaves people at risk of developing diabetes, heart problems, some forms of cancer, and a variety of other health problems. Not everyone who's overweight will have health problems, and many people who are underweight may have these health problems too.

Importantly, the HAES movement reminds us that all people deserve to be treated with kindness and should not be discriminated against because of their size. We should all care about our health more than we care about looking like our favorite celebrities or Instagram influencers.

The problems with diets

They don't work. In fact, you'll probably gain weight.

Let's say you decide to try a low-carb diet. You cut out most bread, pasta, and other grain-based foods from your diet. You'll miss those foods a lot! Assuming you replace those foods with healthy options like fruits and veggies, you'll probably lose weight. For most people (and thousands of people have been studied), the weight loss part of this experience lasts a few months, maybe three months if you're lucky. People will lose a few pounds a week for up to a few months and they'll think the diet is amazing. And then life gets in the way and willpower falls short.

You'll be out to dinner with friends and you won't be able to resist the rolls. Your dad will make your favorite pasta dinner and you'll eat three servings. You'll have a bad day at school and you'll eat a bagel for lunch. Gradually, the carbs will sneak back into your diet (as they should), and gradually, you'll gain whatever weight you lost. Typically, people even gain a bit more weight than they lost. **In studies that follow dieters across time, nearly *all* dieters gain back the weight they lost after two years, and most have gained back extra weight, too.**

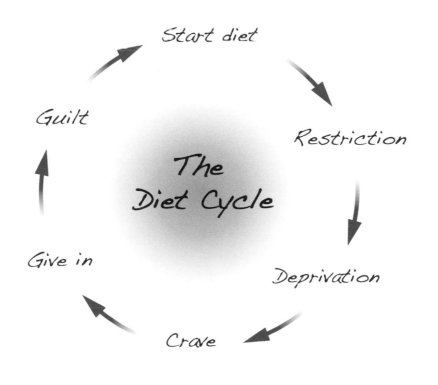

They'll make you cranky

When people go on a diet, they often claim that they want to feel better. People usually expect to feel better both physically and psychologically. Research suggests that people feel good at the start of a diet. They tend to feel like they're committing to do something for themselves that's important.

The problem? These good feelings don't last very long at all, because none of us likes to be deprived. In fact, feeling like we can't eat the foods we want to eat is likely to lead to irritability. Although people often diet to feel better, within a few days they usually feel worse.

One of the first studies to examine how dieting makes people feel took place in the 1940s. The scientists conducting the study reduced the food that participants could eat and people lost weight. That was expected. What wasn't expected was how

this experiment affected the participants' mental health. They became obsessed with food and some even began to dream about food. They had a hard time focusing on regular activities and they became more socially withdrawn, depressed and very, very cranky. Recent studies confirm these early findings: **dieting isn't good for your mental health.**

They encourage body hate

The dieting industry attracts so many customers because it manages to convince us that there is something wrong with our bodies. The industry tells us there is something wrong with us—we're too heavy—but they can help us fix it. Diets focus us on what we shouldn't do (and shouldn't eat) in order to be more attractive. This is an unhealthy way to think about ourselves.

A different way to think about our bodies is in a loving, caring way. We should think about the things we want to do to take care of ourselves, not the things (foods) we want to avoid. Psychologists have actually done research on goal-setting and have found that goals such as this, focusing on what we *do* want to do, are usually easier to achieve than "avoidance goals" (as they're sometimes called). This is a much healthier way to think about our bodies. Avoiding dieting and instead focusing on health make it more likely that we'll think of healthy foods as nourishing our bodies and being a part of self-care. Plus, body hate is a waste of energy and is generally unhelpful.

They use up valuable brain power

Although we all have the potential to keep learning throughout life and to continue getting smarter, our brains can only do so much at a time. Even if you're an excellent multi-tasker, you probably can't cook a meal while reading a book while having a conversation with someone else. You can only think about and do a couple of things at a time. If you're focusing a lot on what you eat—eating being something you likely do throughout the day—this is going to distract from other things that you could (and possibly, should) be doing. Sometimes scientists refer to this as "attentional focus" or "bandwidth." Your ability to focus your attention, or your bandwidth, is limited.

Research suggests that chronic dieters have a hard time completing some tasks, and this also applies to some people who aren't chronic dieters. In scientific studies, dieters have been found to be less able to exhibit self-control than non-dieters, and even less able to speak in front of people than non-dieters. As you grow up and you find yourself tempted by all sorts of diets, it's worth keeping in mind that **deciding to diet means deciding to not be able to do other things**, or to not do other things as well as you could have. Is this a choice you want to make?

Ironic processing

Have you ever tried not to think about something and found that you couldn't get it out of your mind? Maybe you were irritated with a friend and you tried to clear your mind of this irritation to focus on a test at school, but your irritation kept creeping back into your mind. **Ironic processing** is the scientific term used for when you're trying to clear your mind of something but it actually seems to have the opposite effect and you often find yourself thinking about it more. (It's "ironic" because it's the opposite of what you'd expect, and the "processing" part refers to your thoughts or "cognitive processes"). How is this related to dieting? Well, dieting is all about trying to not think about foods that you like and probably want to eat. The more you try to not think about these foods, the more you may actually want them!

Don't believe me? You can try a little experiment on your own. Try not to think about anything chocolately for the next two minutes. You can watch a clock to keep track of time and just sit still, relax, and try not to think about chocolate—cake, cookies, ice cream— put it all out of your mind. How did that turn out?

"What the hell?"

Nope. That's not a typo. Scientists who study dieting have discovered a **"what the hell" effect**. It goes something like this: you decide to go on a diet and limit your sugar intake. You start on Monday, the day that all diets seem to start (the beginning of the week is so hopeful). You're a perfect dieting angel on Monday and Tuesday. Then, on Wednesday, your friend at school upsets you by saying something mean about your shoes. You feel bad and weak willed, so you get a cookie at lunch. Then you get home from school later that day and find some ice cream in the freezer. You haven't given up on your low-sugar diet, but you're craving sugar after not having any for two days. When Thursday rolls around, you have a big science test at school that you stayed up late studying for. You're tired and stressed and you go for a cookie at lunch again. At this point, you say to yourself, "What the hell!" and grab a second cookie. Your short-lived attempt to limit how much sugar you eat is over.

See what happens in situations like this? By trying to eliminate something from your diet, you actually start to want to eat it more. You can successfully limit yourself for a short period of time, maybe two days or even two weeks, but usually you'll say "What the hell" at some point, and you'll end up eating more than if you had never tried to diet in the first place.

This is one of the many ways that dieting can end up being totally counterproductive and unhealthy in the long run.

Diets are part of a "for-profit" industry

Maybe you've heard of "non-profit" organizations. A non-profit organization is an organization that has a goal to help the world in some way, such as the Red Cross, which is dedicated to disaster relief. These organizations don't aim to make money, and any money they obtain through donations or fundraising is used to further the organization's goals.

The diet industry is not a non-profit industry. Many diet plans are described as prescriptions for health and opportunities to feel better. We tend to associate health organizations with non-profit organizations and think of medical providers and medical plans as having the goal of helping us get healthier. But this isn't how diet plans work.

The dieting industry is a multi-billion-dollar industry. People who come up with and sell diet plans don't necessarily care about your health, and they don't necessarily care if you lose weight. If you don't lose weight, you may need their "product" again that much sooner. I know this may sound a bit negative or cynical, but some have gone as far as to say that **the dieting industry is the only profitable industry in the world with a 98% failure rate**.

Keep this in mind the next time you're tempted to diet: there are a lot of people who would be very happy to have you try their diet plans and pay for their book or other services. This doesn't mean they have your best interests in mind.

✓ SUMMING UP #JUSTSAYNOTODIETS

☑ Diets typically don't work and are likely to lead to weight gain over time, not weight loss.

☑ Diets are likely to make you cranky and aren't good for your body image, mental well-being, or physical health.

☑ Focusing on your health, changing your habits slowly, and trying to incorporate more healthy foods like fruits and vegetables into your daily routine are much better for you than dieting.

FIND OUT MORE:

- For more information about the dangers of dieting and how to be smart when it comes to your weight and your health, you can read *Smart People Don't Diet* (2014) by Charlotte Markey. Publisher: Da Capo/ Lifelong Books.

- The Centers for Disease Control and Prevention and the World Health Organization have web pages that include BMI calculators and information about how to understand your weight. Check out: www.cdc. gov/healthyweight/bmi/calculator.html and www.cdc.gov/nccdphp/dnpa/ growthcharts/resources/growthchart.pdf.

- For more information about the Health at Every Size movement, check out *Body Respect: What Conventional Health Books Leave Out, Get Wrong and Just Plain Fail to Understand about Weight* (2014) by Linda Bacon and Lucy Aphramor. Publisher: BenBella Books.

- For more scholarly articles and web pages with information about healthy eating and nutrition, see the companion website for this book: www.TheBodyImageBookforGirls.com.

CHAPTER 7

KEEP FOOD FUN

#LivetoEat

> Humor keeps us alive. Humor and food. Don't forget food. You can go a week without laughing.
>
> Joss Whedon, US screenwriter, director and producer

It would be easy to read Chapters 5 and 6 and start to think that eating can get pretty complicated. Maybe you already thought that. Eating may seem complicated because our scientific understanding is always improving, and with new research we discover more about how to eat to be healthy. But in a lot of ways, **eating isn't—or shouldn't—be complicated**.

> ⇨ **IN THIS CHAPTER, YOU'LL LEARN**
>
> ○ why it's important to be thoughtful about your food choices and to enjoy food,
> ○ what defines eating disorders and how they can develop, and
> ○ how to improve your way of thinking about food and change your habits to support a positive body image.

Balance and moderation

In some ways, healthy eating is very sensible. You eat when you're hungry. You stop eating when you're full. You try to eat a lot of fruits and vegetables and avoid too many sweet and fatty foods. The problem with this logical, healthy advice is that we often feel emotional about food. We crave a cheeseburger when we're hungry. We want our mom's chicken noodle soup when we're sick. We can eat an entire container of Ben and Jerry's ice cream when we're sad. We're not always logical and sensible— sometimes we're emotional.

It's OK to give in to these emotions surrounding food sometimes. An occasional tub of ice cream isn't going to kill you. But a tub of ice cream every day is probably not a good habit. As you get older and you eat more independently—choosing your own lunches at school or making more food choices on your own in general—it's important to try to be balanced and moderate in your choices. By balanced, I mean that you eat a variety of healthy foods and don't overdo the unhealthy foods. By moderate, I mean that you don't take your eating habits to the extremes. Choose fries at school some days, but not every day. Sometimes, when you feel like a cheeseburger, opt for a grilled chicken sandwich. Have a small serving of ice cream some days and an ice cream sundae only rarely.

Live to eat

If you compare the way people eat in some countries (such as the USA) with how people in other countries eat (such as many countries in Europe), it's easy to see that people who eat more don't necessarily enjoy food more. In fact, whereas in many countries the motto seems to be "live to eat," in some of the most overweight countries in the world (for example, the USA) people seem to "eat to live." In other words, people often just eat something when they aren't hungry, or out of boredom, without enjoying the process of meal planning and eating.

The sort of **mindless eating** that people often engage in has some seriously negative consequences: overeating, guilt, and loss of enjoyment surrounding one of life's greatest pleasures—food! Think about it this way: if you sit in front of the television and eat an entire bag of chips while watching a show, you'll no longer be hungry. However, you probably will not have paid very much attention to what you were eating, and you probably wouldn't have savored or enjoyed those chips. (**Savoring** means really noticing and enjoying what you taste.) After eating that entire bag of chips, you may feel too full and guilty about eating so much of something that you know isn't especially healthy. But if you

put a handful of chips
in a bowl and eat them
slowly, and with less
distraction (not in front
of the television), you'd
probably enjoy them a
lot more. Not only would
you have a more positive
eating experience,
you'd probably end up
eating less.

Because we equate
eating with guilt in many
western cultures (such
as the USA and the UK),
and because we spend
a fair amount of energy
worrying about how
much and what we're
eating, we miss out
on a lot of the fun and
enjoyment that food
could bring us. Many
of us have grown up
thinking of some foods
as "good" and some
foods as "bad." I bet you
could list five "good"
and five "bad" foods
without any trouble.
Maybe you'd have milk,
apples, broccoli, carrots,
and Greek yogurt on
your good list. Maybe
you'd have French fries,
pizza, ice cream and sweets on your bad list. But is
food really this straightforward?

There are a number of reasons why it's problematic
to think of foods as "good" and "bad." First of all,
most foods contain many different nutrients, so

they're rarely entirely bad or entirely good. Second, when you feel like a food is bad and forbidden, it often makes you desire that food much more. Imagine what would happen if your mom repeatedly told you that you must eat ice cream for dinner if you wanted broccoli for dessert? You'd probably start to think that broccoli must be pretty awesome if you had to earn it by eating ice cream, and that ice cream must not be all that great. In other words, how we think about and label food can change how much we want it. Also, when we label food as "bad" we're more likely to feel guilty for eating it. This label can change how much we enjoy food—in particular, the foods that are often meant to be special, or parts of celebrations. If your mom makes you a delicious chocolate cake for your birthday, enjoy it and relish this part of celebrating your special day. Don't feel guilty or think of your cake as "bad."

☆ MYTHS AND MISBELIEFS

Organic foods are a necessary part of a healthy diet.

Organic foods can be an important part of a healthy diet, but you don't need to eat only organic foods to have a healthy diet.

Let's back up a bit. What exactly are organic foods? Organic refers to a particular way in which foods such as fruits, vegetables, grains, dairy products, and meat are produced. In order to be considered organic, farmers are required to grow, handle, and process foods in ways that meet environmental and safety goals. For example, they must care for the soil so that they limit pollution and improve the quality of the soil. Farmers are also expected to allow for natural livestock behavior (grazing and eating in a field, and not confining animals only to stalls).

What are the benefits of eating organic foods? They often taste better! Plus, they may be slightly more nutritious, although the science on this is fairly mixed right now. Organic foods are also less likely to be produced using **pesticides** or chemicals (for example, to keep insects from eating plants), so it's less likely that there are any chemicals on these foods.

Perhaps the biggest downside to eating organic is that it can be expensive and challenging to find foods that are only produced organically. Furthermore, most non-organic fruits, vegetables, grains, dairy and meat are a healthy part of any diet. It's much better to eat non-organic strawberries than no strawberries at all. Feel free to eat organic when you can, but you shouldn't feel that it's a necessary part of a healthy diet.

Q & A:

What are GMOs? Are they dangerous? Can they negatively affect my growth and development?

GMOs are genetically modified organisms. In other words, GMOs are living things that have had their genes altered in some way by humans. Usually, when people talk about GMOs, they're referring to plants that are modified as a part of food production, but other organisms are modified to create medicines (such as insulin, which is used to treat diabetes).

People have been modifying their food supply in a variety of ways for hundreds (probably, thousands) of years. Plants have been grown in certain soils, for example, and genes have been "chosen" through the process of breeding (having certain plants or animals fertilize others selected by scientists). It all seems a bit stranger when scientists actually modify genes in a laboratory, but it isn't all that different.

There is no scientific evidence that GMOs are dangerous, or even unhealthy. The American Medical Association, the National Academy of Sciences, the American Association for the Advancement of Science, and the World Health Organization all agree that GMOs are safe. So what's the big deal about GMOs?

Some people worry that there could be risks associated with GMOs that just haven't been revealed yet. And people often fear what they don't totally understand. In fact, one recent scientific study showed that the people most opposed to GMOs were the people who understood them the least.

It's very unlikely that GMOs present any sort of risk or danger to your health, well-being, or development. In fact, by modifying fruits and vegetables, for example, in ways that make them easier to produce and get to us to consume, GMOs may actually help to improve our health overall.

Q & A:

Is food addiction an eating disorder? Can you be addicted to foods like sugar? Can you be a chocoholic?

Food addiction isn't considered an eating disorder by psychologists. Addictions can be extremely serious and even deadly. Usually when psychologists discuss addictions, they mean addictions to chemicals or substances like nicotine found in cigarettes, alcohol, or drugs. Regular overuse of these substances can affect nearly every part of the body and result in a physical dependency on them. In other words, once a person is used to regular drug use, for example, they'll experience withdrawal symptoms when the drug use stops. The person comes to need the drug, and without it they may experience symptoms ranging from flu-like symptoms and seizures to headaches and shaking. Although reducing consumption of a food you're used to eating regularly may result in cravings, it's unlikely to result in these sorts of serious physical withdrawal symptoms.

It's possible to be in the habit of eating a lot of sugar and to crave it. It's possible to like chocolate so much that you think of yourself as a chocoholic. Some research does suggest that similar areas of the brain are involved when a person eats a food they crave and when a person uses a drug. But this doesn't mean that "addiction" to food is the same thing as addiction to a drug. It's typically easier to change an eating habit than it is to change a drug habit, for example. As I've discussed more in Chapter 6 and in this chapter, habits can be persistent. But food also has a nourishing and important role in sustaining our health. The same cannot be said of other truly addictive substances.

We want it fast—and supersized

In many western countries, people are extreme in their desire to get food quickly. Instead of enjoying the process of planning and selecting what we're going to eat, people want food fast. This explains the popularity of fast food. For example, according to the Centers for Disease Control and Prevention, more than one in three Americans eat **fast food** on any given day.

Maybe you're wondering what's wrong with wanting our food fast. Fast isn't always bad; sometimes we're really hungry! But getting food from a drive-through, eating in our cars, and eating food prepared outside the home (which tends to be less healthy) on a regular basis aren't the best habits. Eating fast food tends to contribute to mindless eating and rarely lends itself to sit-down, family-style dinners and savoring our food.

In addition to wanting our food fast, we also tend to want as much as we can get for as little money as possible (this is also a part of why fast food is popular). We tend to value quantity (how much) over quality (how good/nutritious the food is), and it's easy to get a meal "supersized" at a fast food restaurant. Of course you don't have to eat all the food given to you at any restaurant, but research suggests that bigger portion sizes lead people to end up eating more. It's better for you to eat healthy, tasty, fresh food in smaller quantities than it is to eat a lot of food that isn't particularly healthy, tasty or fresh.

Reminder: Be careful not to restrict yourself too much

It's important to enjoy food and eating while eating healthy foods. It's equally important not to be too rigid about your food choices. As I discussed in Chapter 6, it can backfire if you spend too much energy trying to avoid the foods you love.

There are a variety of potentially negative consequences of restricting yourself from eating foods you enjoy. Aside from not being able to enjoy food, you may miss out on much more, because food has important cultural meanings. A birthday cake or a wedding cake is often considered an important part of a celebration. A big turkey or ham dinner is an important part of Thanksgiving or Christmas gatherings. Hotdogs, hamburgers, and pie can be favorite parts of a backyard barbecue in the summer. These gatherings and celebrations are about the delicious foods, the time spent with loved ones, the holidays, and the memories made. Of course, you can go to a barbecue and not eat a hotdog. However, if you spend the entire gathering avoiding hotdogs, feeling deprived, and wishing you could eat a hotdog, you aren't going to have a lot of fun. At the extreme, consistent **food restriction** can lead to the development of an eating disorder.

Fasting, binging, and everything in between

You've probably heard about eating disorders from the media or in a health class at school. You may not realize that there are several different kinds of eating disorders, and that eating disorders can be *really* serious. In fact, they're the most deadly of any mental illness. Let's consider the most common eating disorders.

Anorexia nervosa

Anorexia nervosa, usually referred to as anorexia, is an eating disorder that's relatively rare, but extremely serious. Individuals who develop anorexia typically eat very little and often eat only certain types of foods. They may exercise excessively and tend to be obsessed with food, calories, and other qualities of foods, such as how much fat is in different types of food. Anorexic patients are usually concerned with trying to lose weight and tend to experience extreme body image concerns, although they very often are not overweight. Although individuals with anorexia are often seriously underweight, an individual can be overweight and still be anorexic; you can't always determine who has an eating disorder by looking at a person.

The health consequences of anorexia can be very serious. When the body doesn't get enough of the nutrients it needs, a variety of problems may develop in addition to dramatic weight loss. Some of the many health concerns that can develop include stomach pain, weakness, lowered immune functioning (the body's ability to fight illness is reduced), slower heart rate, overall feelings of coldness and difficulty with temperature regulation, difficulty sleeping, dizziness and fainting, difficulty concentrating, loss of menstrual periods, and even death.

Q & A:

I understand that people with anorexia often skip meals or eat very small meals, and that anorexia is a very dangerous disorder. But I've also read about people who use "intermittent fasting" for weight loss, which seems similar to skipping meals. What's the difference? And does intermittent fasting work?

Intermittent fasting has received attention in recent years as an approach to weight loss. It typically involves people eating as they regularly do for 5 days a week and then eating relatively little for a couple of days a week. Some people eat within a select window of time each day—for example, between 10 am and 5 pm. The general idea isn't to limit the food eaten overall, but to reduce what is eaten to certain periods of time.

Research by nutritionists suggests that intermittent fasting can help people lose weight, but not any better than just changing the foods people eat (for example, eating more fruit and fewer unhealthy snacks) or exercising more often. One of the biggest problems with intermittent fasting is that it leaves people hungry. It's a way of eating that can be difficult for people to stick to long term. In other words, even if it helps people lose weight, they're likely to gain that weight back over time.

How is intermittent fasting different from an eating disorder? This is a good and complicated question. If someone is intermittently fasting because she is worried about her weight, avoids social situations so that it's easier to avoid food, feels concerned about her body size or shape, and has lost a lot of weight recently, then it's likely that this person has taken fasting way too far and has developed an eating disorder. If someone sometimes skips breakfast in the hope of losing weight, that's probably not an eating disorder.

Because intermittent fasting and eating disorders share some similar characteristics, I would never recommend that a child or an adolescent try this approach to weight loss. In fact, this could be an especially bad approach to weight loss for young people who are still growing and experiencing puberty, because they consistently need a variety of nutrients to stay healthy. I'm not a fan of it for adults, either.

Bulimia nervosa

Bulimia nervosa, or "bulimia," typically involves **binging** and then **purging** food. When someone binges, they eat *much* more than is typical in one sitting. You may feel really full if you eat three or four pieces of pizza, but a real binge would mean eating an entire pizza plus more, in most cases. Bulimic individuals tend to feel a loss of control and an inability to stop eating when they binge. After a binge, a bulimic person usually feels not just full but guilty, and then engages in some sort of purge. Purging can take different forms, including using medication that leads them to vomit or get diarrhea, or by exercising extensively.

The health consequences of bulimia are somewhat similar to the consequences of anorexia. In both disorders, individuals are unlikely to get the nutrients they need. Furthermore, for both anorexic and bulimic people, the time and energy focused on food and weight is a major distraction from the rest of their lives. But unlike anorexic individuals, bulimic people often develop problems with their stomachs and digestive systems as a result of binging and purging. They also may have difficulty sleeping, difficulty concentrating, problems fighting infection, muscle weakness, and

irregularities with their periods. Purging may result in other health concerns, including dental problems and very serious issues including chemical imbalances. These sorts of imbalances can lead to complications including death, often without any warning.

Binge eating disorder

Binge eating disorder (aka BED) is thought to be the most common eating disorder. Individuals with BED tend to binge (at least once a week for at least three months) without purging. Binges are described as excessive in terms of how much is eaten, and they're experienced as uncontrollable. When people binge, they often describe the experience as if they're in a trance. They eat quickly and until they're uncomfortable and then feel guilty and ashamed afterwards.

People with BED often experience problems with their stomachs and digestive systems. They may get cramps, constipation, heartburn, or other symptoms as a result of their problematic eating habits. They often spend a lot of time and energy thinking about food and what they will eat. People with BED are at risk of being overweight or obese and may experience stigma and shame as a result of their body size.

Unspecified feeding or eating disorder

Sometimes people have unhealthy eating habits that are not as severe as anorexia, bulimia, or binge eating disorder, but their eating habits still disrupt their life. Their habits may lead to drastic weight gain or weight loss. Most importantly, these people are stressed out about their eating, body image or weight (or all three). These individuals are often diagnosed with having an **unspecified feeding or eating disorder**.

To receive an official diagnosis of anorexia, for example, patients must have a number of specific symptoms. A patient may fall just short of the required number of symptoms, but they may clearly have serious concerns and unhealthy behaviors surrounding food. This patient would likely get diagnosed as having an unspecified feeding or eating disorder. This diagnosis helps different healthcare providers to realize the seriousness of the patient's symptoms and can help organize treatment for the patient.

Body dysmorphic disorder

Body dysmorphic disorder (aka BDD) is not an eating disorder, but often co-occurs with eating disorders. In other words, people who have eating disorders sometimes have BDD, but just having BDD is not an eating disorder.

BDD is actually a body image disorder. People with BDD are preoccupied with their body's defects and flaws. They are compulsive about tending to their appearance and may go to extremes to alter their appearance, such as obtaining extensive cosmetic surgery. At the heart of BDD is the inability of people to see themselves as others do and to be extremely critical of themselves. People with BDD may experience not only self-doubt, but also **anxiety** and **depression** as a result of their preoccupation with their bodies.

MYTHS AND MISBELIEFS

You can never eat too healthily.

Eating healthy foods is a good way to take care of your body. However, it is possible to become concerned with eating too healthily. If you find yourself spending a lot of time thinking about what you are eating and feel guilty if you eat anything that is remotely unhealthy, you may have what is referred to sometimes as **orthorexia**. The **American Psychological Association** does not recognize orthorexia as a clinical disorder, but it is a term used to describe an overconcern with eating healthfully, avoidance of unhealthy foods, a rigidity about food choice, and often body image concerns. People with orthorexia often experience anxiety and obsessive-compulsive tendencies. Although you may benefit physically from a focus on healthy foods, taken to the extreme this can become problematic psychologically. Food should be enjoyed! Every meal does not need to include avocado, kale, and almonds.

How does a person develop an eating disorder?

As with any mental health problem, no one wants to develop an eating disorder. It is possible that a person may have concerns about their body image or weight, but this doesn't mean they want to develop a serious disorder. It's important to keep this in mind if you encounter a friend or someone you know who has an eating disorder (see the Q&A below).

There are many factors that can contribute to the development of an eating disorder. Usually, people who develop eating disorders are concerned about their weight and don't feel good about their bodies. Sometimes they're overweight, but more often they're not overweight, but are still worried about what they eat and how they look. It turns out that usually a person's actual weight is much less relevant than a person's feelings about their weight in the development of eating disorders.

MY STORY

Serena Nicole, 21 years old

When I was younger (from about 12 to 16 years old), I was extremely self-conscious about my body. I was skinny and looked like a young boy with a bad haircut and a totally flat chest. Among my friends, I was the skinniest, and people would always make condescending comments to me about my body and how I looked. I got used to hearing, "You're so pretty, even though you're so skinny," or "Why are you so skinny? You must not eat enough." The ironic thing is that I actually ate a lot.

One memory from my early teens especially stands out to me. On my 14th birthday, I was wearing a bikini at my pool party and I was taking turns taking goofy pictures with all my friends. After everyone else left, my best friend and I were looking back at all of the pictures. We didn't even make it through half of the pictures before she staged an "intervention." She began telling me that she was so sorry for being such a bad friend and not noticing sooner that I had a problem. She was convinced that I had an eating disorder! Just for the record, I never did. After a few minutes, she calmed down and apologized for how she reacted. She said that she never really noticed how skinny I actually was. After that birthday, I found myself double checking myself in the mirror or in pictures; all of a sudden, I became so self-conscious about my body.

Just recently, I feel like I am finally coming to terms with my body. I'm even starting to feel happy with my body, who I am, and how I look. I feel like it's a mindset of acceptance that I've finally obtained and it's allowing me to truly be happy with who I am. I also think that surrounding myself with positive people has been really helpful to me. It can take time to find the people who lift you up, bring out the best in you, and want what is best for you.

I wish I had realized sooner how important it is to accept yourself—and express yourself. I've learned to dress how I want to and be comfortable with showing people who I really am. If anyone says anything negative to me about my looks, I just tell myself that they must be jealous. Haters are always gonna hate. But that's not who I want to be.

Many people who develop eating disorders live in families that talk a lot about food and dieting, or in which others have eating disorder symptoms themselves. Sometimes family members may tease and make a person feel bad about their food choices or weight.

Media influences are also relevant to individuals' development of eating disorders. As discussed in earlier chapters (see Chapter 4), images of beauty often feature very slender women (and men). Messages about the importance of weight, and being thin, are everywhere in western cultures. It's easy for people to start to believe that they'll be happier if they're a certain weight, and to be willing to take drastic measures to achieve that weight. The problem is that there are so many serious health problems associated with not maintaining healthy eating habits. An eating disorder may contribute to weight loss, but will cause many other problems.

Some research even suggests that people with certain personalities may be more vulnerable to developing eating disorders. People who are perfectionists or anxious are more likely to worry about things like fitting in with their peers and looking a certain way. This may lead them to be more at risk of developing an eating disorder. All the factors that contribute to the development of eating disorders are likely influenced by our biology; some people possess biological characteristics that place them at risk. But there are many other factors that may make one person more likely to develop an eating disorder than another person, so they're not doomed by their biology. These are complex disorders, and they're very serious. Regardless of the factors that contribute to the development of an eating disorder for any one individual, it isn't the individual's fault that they're sick.

Individuals suffering from an eating disorder usually require treatment by several healthcare professionals including physicians, psychologists, and nutritionists. Early treatment is often more effective than waiting to see if a person grows out of an eating disorder. It's always safer to provide too much help and support to a person than not enough help and support.

You know you haven't been eating enough healthy food and you want to do better

Even if you're certain that you don't have anything resembling an eating disorder, you may find yourself wanting to improve your eating habits as you read this book. As far as eating habits go, I think we're all works in progress. Most of us could stand to improve our eating habits at least a little bit. There are so many food temptations that can pull us off the path of healthy eating: vending machines, drive-throughs, and even options available in the cafeteria at school. Because what we eat has a significant impact on our health, it can be a good decision to work toward improvements to our eating habits. Where should you start?

It's difficult to change any sort of habit, including any health habit, such as what you eat. In Chapter 6, I discussed some good ways to work on eating more healthfully. One of the most important things to do is to work with your current life to make lasting changes. Think about the ways that your surroundings—your family, school, and friends—influence what you eat. If you feel like you could alter a habit at home, maybe eating healthier breakfasts,

Q & A:

I have a good friend who I think has an eating disorder. She's constantly talking about food and her weight, and she exercises for hours every day. I know that exercise can be good for you, but I think she's taking it too far. What should I do?

It's likely that at some point in your life you'll know at least one person who has an eating disorder. It's important to think about how best to be helpful in these situations. First of all, you probably want to choose whether or not you want to talk to your friend directly, or to talk to an adult who may be able to help. It may make sense to do both. If you aren't comfortable approaching your friend directly, you could talk to one of her parents, a psychologist, counselor, or teacher at your school. Sharing your concern with a caring adult can help to ease your worry and allow someone else to step in and help.

If you're comfortable talking with your friend directly, you want to be careful not to approach her by blaming her for her problem. No one wants to develop an eating disorder; she has an illness similar to other kinds of physical illnesses. It's often helpful to try to have a calm conversation that allows you to express your concern and worry about her. You may want to direct her to some helpful resources online, such as the eating disorders screening tool on the National Eating Disorders Association website (www.nationaleatingdisorders.org/screening-tool). You may want to let her know that you're aware that eating disorders can be very serious—even deadly—and that you care about her getting better and enjoying food and having a healthy future. Consider helping her to find a way to get professional help. It can be scary for people to ask for help, even though it's probably a good idea for her to talk with her doctor and a psychologist. At the very least, she could call the National Eating Disorders helpline (USA: 1-800-931-2237) or the Beat Eating Disorders helpline (UK: 0808 801 0677).

Sometimes people who need medical help aren't ready to get it. It's possible that you could talk with your friend and she may not follow your advice at all. Try not to take this personally, but continue to express your concern to your friend. Most importantly, don't ever shame someone or make them feel bad for having a problem. This is unlikely to help and may only damage your relationship with the person.

then talk with your family about how to do this together. If you're always tempted to make a poor choice in the cafeteria at school, you could make a pact with a friend to try to avoid juice and opt for water. If you and your friends always go out for pizza on the weekends, you may want to suggest other options once in a while.

For some people, improving eating habits may mean eating different types of things, like more vegetables and less fried food. For others, it may mean eating more food. It can be difficult to eat intuitively, or eat when you're hungry and stop when you're full, but this is a valuable thing to think about and practice for the rest of your life. Many experts believe that, although it's worthwhile to be thoughtful about our food choices, it's even more important not to worry about food and eating. Most—although not all—of us in the USA and Europe are lucky enough to have enough food to keep us alive, and this is what's most important. Food is the fuel that keeps our bodies working. It's good to give our body healthy fuel, but there is nothing wrong with enjoying all sorts of foods and even indulging in unhealthy foods.

How you eat is related to how you feel

How you eat—even how you think about food—has a big impact on many areas of your life. Part of the connection between how you eat and how you feel is physical; both your brain and your body react to what you eat (or don't eat). If you aren't eating enough and you're hungry, you're also more likely to be tired, unable to concentrate, and maybe even **hangry** (hungry + angry). If you're not eating healthily, you may also find yourself feeling a lack of energy, being easily distracted, and finding it difficult to learn. Poor nutrition is also associated with an inability to fight off illness and infection, which is part of why people in poor, developing countries are more likely to struggle with health problems not found in wealthier countries.

Your eating habits are also likely to affect how you feel about yourself and your psychological health, even if you never have anything resembling an eating disorder. For example, in one recent study, researchers found that lower self-esteem seems to be associated with poorer eating habits. This may mean that people with low self-esteem don't eat as many healthy foods, or it may mean that eating healthy foods has a positive impact on people's self-esteem. Most likely, both

of these things are partly true.

In related research, an association has been found between self-compassion, eating behaviors, and body image. What is **self-compassion**? Well, if you're compassionate, you're concerned about others and you show them sympathy. Self-compassion is treating yourself with this same sort of concern and sympathy. People who think of themselves with kindness and caring are more likely to have more intuitive eating habits than people who think poorly of themselves. Self-compassion is also linked to a positive body image. This is just one more reason to treat yourself like you would a good friend.

✔ SUMMING UP #LIVETOEAT

✓ Healthy eating habits include choosing mostly healthy food options from what is available to you (for example, fruits and vegetables), but also include enjoying food and making it a fun part of your life.

✓ Always restricting yourself from eating foods you enjoy isn't healthy and may lead to disordered eating, or even a serious eating disorder. If you think that you or someone you know may have an eating disorder, talk with an adult and look for treatment as soon as possible.

✓ It's OK to think about improving your eating habits by including more healthy choices into what you usually eat. But it's not OK to worry about what you eat!

FIND OUT MORE:

- If you have questions about eating disorders, you should spend some time on the National Eating Disorders and Beat Eating Disorders' websites, available at: www.nationaleatingdisorders.org and https://www. beateatingdisorders.org.uk.

- If you are interested in learning more about GMOs, you may want to read recent articles published in the health section of the *New York Times*, such as: www.nytimes.com/2019/01/15/well/eat/gmo-foods-genetically-modified-knowledge.html.

- Learn more about self-compassion by reading Dr. Kristin Neff's website, available at: https://self-compassion.org/.

- For more scholarly articles and web pages with information about healthy eating and nutrition, see the companion website for this book: www.TheBodyImageBookforGirls.com.

CHAPTER 8

MAKE YOUR BODY WORK FOR YOU

#BeFit

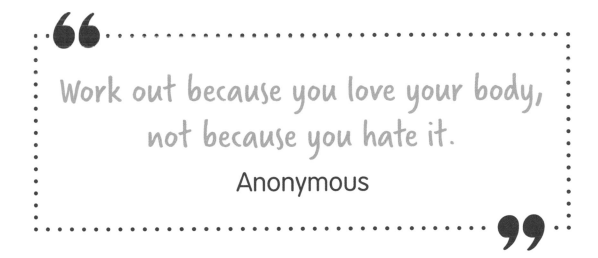

> Work out because you love your body,
> not because you hate it.
>
> Anonymous

As you've probably noticed by now, a theme in this book is that it's important to take really good care of your body. **One way to care for your body, and to keep it working for you, is to be physically active.**

What is the difference between physical activity, exercise, and fitness?

Physical activity is pretty much any kind of movement of your body. Nearly anything that requires energy to do is physical activity: walking, running, playing basketball, swimming, mowing the lawn, and even cleaning your bedroom. **Exercise** is a particular type of physical activity that's usually more planned and purposeful. In other words, playing on your school's volleyball team is exercise: you do it regularly, it's structured, and you intend to be doing it. On the other hand, you probably don't clean your room with the intention of "getting exercise."

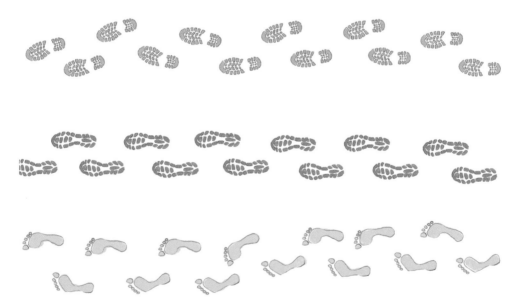

Often people talk about engaging in physical activity or exercise with the goal of being fit. **Fitness** is a broad term with more than one definition. Often the way people talk about fitness is in terms of getting in shape. What counts as fitness for one person may look very different for another person. The word fitness has become popular in recent years, as has the word **fitspiration** (aka "fitspo"). Fitspiration refers to images, **memes**, or ideas, usually shared on social media, that are supposed to inspire fitness. Unfortunately, there is some research to suggest that fitspiration isn't actually always inspiring. In fact, sometimes seeing other fit (usually slender and toned) people just makes us feel bad about ourselves. Feeling bad about ourselves or feeling inferior to other people is rarely motivating.

IN THIS CHAPTER, YOU'LL LEARN

○ about the benefits of physical activity for your body image and your health in general,

○ how much you should aim to be active, and the importance of balancing this with getting enough sleep and limiting other activities such as screen time, and

○ techniques for establishing good health habits for physical activity or anything else that could benefit your health.

How much activity is ideal?

Any kind of movement is good for you, and obsessing over how much you move is usually not, so it's best not to get hung up on numbers too much. However, the US Department of Health and Human Services recommends that kids aged 6–17 years engage in **1 hour of physical activity a day**. That may sound like a lot, but remember that physical activity can include all sorts of things. If you walk to school, or even walk around while you're at school, you may easily find yourself active for 30 minutes most days.

Some of the activity you take part in is likely to be aerobic. If you're working up a sweat and breathing heavily, either because you ran up some stairs at school or because you've gone for a jog at home, then this is aerobic activity. Even a fast-paced walk is aerobic activity. But it's valuable to also take part in physical activity that's good for your muscles and bones. This can include stretching and working on flexibility, doing push-ups or sit-ups, and even lifting weights as you get older.

☆ MYTHS AND MISBELIEFS

Following fitness experts on Instagram will help motivate you to exercise regularly and get in shape.

Who doesn't like to feel inspired? Most people can use some inspiration (or "fitspiration") to help them maintain good health habits, including regular physical activity. However, fitness experts on Instagram or other forms of social media may not be the best place to turn for advice and inspiration. Usually, fitness "experts" are incredibly toned, slim, and do little more than work on their fitness. That's their job! In contrast, you most likely go to school, study, hang out with your friends, and participate in other activities like your school's debating team, basketball team, or French club. You don't have time to exercise all day long, and you have other important activities to prioritize. What this means is that fitness experts aren't usually a good source of comparison (or inspiration) because you're likely to feel like you don't measure up to these experts and that you never will.

When we compare ourselves to others and this results in us feeling worse about ourselves, this is one form of social comparison. Scientists refer to this particular kind of social comparison as upward social comparison. We're comparing ourselves with others who are "above" us or are more accomplished than us in some way. The result is that we usually feel bad about ourselves. In fact, in one recent study examining women in their 20s, exposure to fitspiration images on social media was linked to higher rates of eating disorder symptoms. In other words, in this study, women not only felt bad about themselves after viewing what were intended to be inspirational images, but they may have been more likely to adopt unhealthy eating habits as well. Turns out fitspiration is just not usually all that inspirational.

What are the benefits of physical activity?

Why try to be regularly active? There is a great deal of scientific research to suggest that regular physical activity is good for both your psychological and physical health. Kids who are physically active tend to be more fit and have stronger bones and muscles. Being regularly physically active is also associated with better mental health—for example, lower rates of depression. Being physically active may even be good for your brain and your ability to learn.

Perhaps most important, though, is that kids who are regularly active tend to develop an appreciation for how good they feel when they move their bodies or participate in team sports. They're more likely to develop good habits that they stick with as they get older. If you develop a love for swimming when you're young, you're more likely to swim as a form of exercise when you're an adult. We all become more vulnerable to health problems as we get older, including heart disease, type 2 diabetes, and cancer. Being active can help prevent some of these health problems and may even help us live longer lives.

MY STORY

Leslie Patricia, 21 years old

Since I was young, I've always had a love/hate relationship with my body. On the one hand, I've always loved how athletic my body can look while I'm being active and working out. There are days where I look at myself and think, "You know what? I look good and I don't care what anyone else thinks." On the other hand, I've struggled with not being as skinny as some other girls. I've always had more muscle, and as I've gotten older, I've put on more weight and muscle.

A lot of my thoughts and ideas about my body have changed within the last year. Instead of forcing myself to look a certain way by counting calories and forcing myself into the gym when I'm absolutely exhausted, I've started to wear things that flatter my body and make me feel confident. For example, this summer when I was trying on bathing suits in a store, I decided to focus on how great I looked in a one-piece bathing suit instead of hating how I looked in a bikini. I've never thought about my body in that way before. It had always been, "Oh well, I'll buy this and then I can lose weight and wear it." But now, if something doesn't fit the way I want, I don't tell myself I'm "too fat"; I instead tell myself that the article of clothing I just tried on wasn't made for my body type.

In the past few years, my boyfriend has been really supportive when it comes to my body image. Whenever I've been down about how I've looked, he'll say to me, "I can respect how you feel, but I want you to know, when I look at you, that's not what I see. I think you look great." This has been a great help to me. Instead of shutting me down and telling me that I'm "wrong," he will validate how I feel, but then tell me instead what he sees and that he doesn't agree. A lot of my friends are also encouraging and supportive. Sometimes you just need a friend to help boost your confidence when you're feeling down on yourself.

I wish I could tell my younger self that everyone has a different body type and that's OK. I wish I had learned to stop comparing myself to others a long time ago. It can be hard to remember that the rich and famous people and all those fitness gurus on Instagram don't really look the way they seem to.

Ninety-nine percent of pictures that these people post are photoshopped and filtered.

I'm glad to know that I'm not alone in struggling a bit with my body image. I know it's really common, but it's something I can work on. These days, I'm trying to focus on what I really do like about myself and my body. For example, I love my eyes, freckles, and legs. These are three things about myself that I would never change.

There's a difference between trying to look like someone else and having goals for yourself.

Finding what you love

I'm guessing that some of you reading this book will feel like you're not sure how to work physical activity into your life because you just don't like sports or don't feel like you're very good at any of them. I can relate to this. I was always chosen last for teams when I was a kid. I wasn't particularly athletic and I always felt self-conscious when I tried to play sports. I wasn't against being physically active, but I just felt stressed out by even the thought of playing sports.

Fortunately, being physically active doesn't have to mean that you play a sport. There are a lot of ways to get yourself moving. Here are some ideas, in ABC order: acrobatics, ballet, cycling, dance, exercise classes, fencing, gymnastics, horseback riding, ice skating, jumping rope, kickboxing, line dancing, martial arts, netball, Oztag (a type of rugby), pilates, quoits, rock climbing, stretching, tai chi, ultimate frisbee,

acrobatics

volleyball, walking, Xtreme paintball, **yoga**, and zumba. Many people end up trying a lot of different activities before they find something they love. At different stages in your life, you may try out different activities. Right now, being on your school's dance team or swim team may be a lot of fun and good exercise, but as you get older you may find yourself riding a bike to school or walking your dog to get exercise.

It's valuable to think outside the box when it comes to ways to move your body. Maybe you'll find that you love gardening or enjoy playing tennis with a friend. You don't have to be competitive (or even social) to be physically active, and there are an endless number of options. Be creative in thinking about ways to keep your body fit and make it work for you.

Why being active can make you feel good about your body

In the past, boys participated in sports much more than girls did. This is changing, with girls starting to participate in all sorts of sports ranging from soccer to swimming and track events. Unfortunately, girls

participate in sports only about half as often as boys
do. I say "unfortunately" because there are so many
benefits to being regularly active with a group of
other people—everything from learning new skills to
having fun with friends can be valuable. And there is
evidence that physical activity can increase positive
feelings about your body.

You may recall the discussion of body **functionality**
from Chapter 3. Basically, the idea is that girls tend
to focus on how their bodies look far too often and
instead should focus on how their bodies work or
function. You probably see so many advertisements
for beauty products—make-up, hair products,
skin products, and perfume—that you hardly even
think about them. However, all these products
focus on your appearance and how to change
it. This all comes at a cost, both the price of the
products themselves and the time and energy to
use them. However, they may limit how you can
move or function, whether because your shoes are
uncomfortable or because you don't want your
hair to get messed up. The focus is all about how
you look, whereas participation in sports and other
physical activities leads to a focus on how you move.
Exercising regularly so you can run or swim faster
may take time, but it's also a good way to improve
your health and fitness. And it's fun to see how much
you can improve at an activity over time.

Scientific studies support the idea that focusing on
functionality through participation in sports and
other kinds of physical activities can be good for
how girls think about their bodies. Girls who are

athletes have been found to have higher self-esteem than girls who aren't athletes. Female university-age athletes have also been found to feel more appreciation of their bodies and to actually report valuing how their bodies function more than non-athletes. A big study also found that girls who are athletes have more overall positive body images than non-athletes. This doesn't mean that you need to be an athlete to reap the rewards of physical activity. Remember, any sort of movement counts as physical activity! And any movement that you do regularly can help you think more about the many amazing things that your body can *do*, which is way more valuable than how your body looks.

Establishing good habits

Maybe, as you read this chapter, the idea of participating in more physical activity is growing on you. How do you get into the habit of being more active? It's typically difficult for people to change their habits, but there are some evidence-based practices that will help.

First of all, don't aim too high. That may sound sort of pessimistic, but it's just too easy to set an unreasonable fitness goal and then find it impossible and give up all together. Set a small goal that you know that you can achieve. Maybe your goal is to walk your dog for 10 minutes each day. Or to take a dance class with a friend each week. Do something that will be fairly easy. Once you do this new activity for a few weeks, consider adding another change. Maybe you walk your dog for 15 minutes per day or maybe you run with your dog instead of walking her. Maybe you add in a second dance class per week. When you set small, achievable goals and you're successful, that success will motivate you to do more. If it doesn't, then reconsider your goals. Maybe you don't really like dance. Maybe you'd rather go to a gym instead of walking your dog.

Another important thing to consider if you're trying to add in physical activity to your regular routine is that this may mean you have to take something else out of your regular routine. As the saying goes, there are only so many hours in the day. If your schedule is already packed full, you may need to drop something to add in physical activity. Be sure you don't drop other valuable activities like spending enough time on your homework or getting enough sleep.

Telling people about your goals and asking for help in achieving them can also be helpful. Sometimes scientists call this a **commitment strategy**. We tend to be more likely to stick with a goal if other people know about it. We don't want to feel embarrassed if others realize we didn't stick with our goal. It can also be valuable to ask people for help in meeting our goals. Maybe you'd like a parent or a friend to remind you of your activity goals, or maybe you want a friend to exercise with you. Either way, it can be useful to have supportive people in your life helping you achieve any of the goals that you have.

Finally, be patient with yourself and don't give up. If you don't follow through with whatever activity goal you've set for yourself, this doesn't mean you throw in the towel forever. Maybe your life feels too busy right now, but once summer rolls around you'll have more time and you can work on setting new activity goals. Once you establish a habit for 2–3 months it tends to stick, but you have to keep at it before the sticking happens. People tend to be creatures of habit, and changing those habits isn't easy. Be patient with yourself if you don't meet your goals the first time you try. Most people have to try more than once to change any habit.

Try taking it outside

One thing that may help you stick to a physical activity regimen is to try exercising outside. A number of scientific studies have examined how people feel about exercise that's done outside versus inside. Usually, participants in this research are asked to do something like go for a walk outside or walk on a treadmill inside. Not only do people tend to say that they like walking outside more, but they even report feeling less tense and less depressed after a walk outside. The same doesn't seem to be true of walking on a treadmill. People seem to find outdoor physical activity easier, too. Walking on a treadmill is a good way to get some exercise, but if you don't enjoy it that much, it'll be hard to stick with it. The trick to being regularly active is to find something that you like enough to keep doing.

If being outside might make physical activity more pleasurable, what else can you do outside? In addition to walking, running and hiking are great outdoor activities. Nearly any sport can be played outside, too. Biking, football, and basketball are all possible outdoor activities. However, if the weather or other circumstances don't allow you to exercise outdoors, you should still try to find ways to move indoors. In research comparing people's moods after they sit around indoors versus exercise indoors, the folks who were active almost always seemed to be in a better mood and felt more relaxed than the people who were sitting around, even if they were allowed to play on a computer while they sat.

Q & A:

I've heard a lot about high-intensity interval training (HIIT) recently. What is it, and is it a good idea?

High-intensity interval training (or HIIT) has received a lot of attention in recent years, probably because people like the idea of training hard ("high intensity") for short periods of time. Usually, HIIT workouts involve alternating between nearly all-out exertion (for example, running as absolutely fast as you can) and lower exertion (for example, jogging) for intervals of a minute or so each. Sometimes the high-intensity parts of the workout last for 30 seconds and the lower-intensity parts last for a few minutes; there are no set rules, really. The idea is to push yourself for short periods of time, and the total length of the workout is often under 30 minutes.

There is some evidence that HIIT workouts can be a good way to increase your fitness and are at least as good as longer workouts at a mid-level of exertion (for example, running at a medium pace for you). Some fitness experts have suggested that HIIT workouts burn more fat than regular workouts, but a recent review of the scientific research suggests that this may not always be the case. If you enjoy interval training, then work it into your exercise routine. But if you don't, then don't worry about it. Any kind of physical activity is typically good for you.

Can you exercise too much?

Watching professional athletes and people who enjoy being active can be so inspiring. It can make you want to devote more of your time and energy to achieving your own fitness potential. Physical activity is incredibly good for your body and your mind, but as with anything, there can be too much of a good thing.

In terms of the physical, some research suggests that participating in regular, vigorous exercise, such as jogging, can add 5–6 years onto your lifespan. However, other research suggests that it may be better to be more moderate in your approach to exercise (for example, not exercising every day) to reap the most benefit in terms of how long you live. Even with some inconsistencies in the science, it's safe to conclude that exercise is nearly always good for you physically. However, it's important to listen to your body. If you're tired all the time, really hungry from exercising, or not enjoying exercising anymore, then you're probably overdoing it.

Q & A:

Can I get too muscular from exercising?

Regular exercise can lead to your body looking different, and you certainly may acquire some muscle mass. In other words, where there was once fat, you may now see more muscles and definition. Most people like these changes in their body; they're proof of time spent exercising, and they look good.

It's probably mostly a matter of opinion whether it's possible for girls and women to become too muscular. What is too muscular? Because of differences in girls' and boys' hormones following puberty (see Chapter 2), girls and women are less likely to develop the big, bulky muscles that boys and men may develop. Furthermore, in order to develop a lot of muscle mass, you would need to spend a fair amount of time lifting pretty heavy weights. Cardiovascular exercises like running or swimming are very unlikely to lead to the development of a lot of muscle mass.

The short answer to this question is probably no. It's also important to remember that muscles are about a lot more than how you look. They mean that you're strong, and strength means that can probably do a lot of useful things: carrying your own groceries or shopping bags at the mall, mowing the lawn, climbing up a flight of stairs without getting winded, and lifting heavy objects, are just a few examples.

It also seems pretty clear that too much exercise can have a negative effect on your mental health. This is especially true if exercising feels like an obligation and not like something that you enjoy. Psychologists sometimes refer to exercise that feels necessary, especially more than one time per day, as **compulsive exercise**. If you feel like you're scheduling your day around exercise, worrying about how much you exercise, not eating unless you exercise a certain amount, or feeling guilty if you don't exercise, you may be a compulsive exerciser. Compulsive exercise can be dangerous for your mental health and you should talk to someone—a parent, school counselor, or therapist—if you think this describes you. **Being regularly physically active can be great, but if you end up pushing yourself all the time and not feeling like you're enjoying your activity, it's time to step back and rethink things.**

And make sure you rest, too

It's important to your health that you keep your body moving, but it's equally important that you make sure your body gets enough rest. Did you know that more than half of all middle schoolers and high schoolers in the USA don't get enough sleep? How much sleep do you get on most nights? Think about what time you usually get into bed, when you usually fall asleep, and when you usually wake up. Are you sleeping at least 8 or 9 hours each night?

The Centers for Disease Control and Prevention recommends that 6–12-year-olds need 9–12 hours of sleep each night, and 13–18-year-olds need 8–10 hours of sleep each night. Sleep is related to pretty much every aspect of your health and well-being.

Although the relationship between sleep and different sorts of diseases is complicated, not getting enough sleep may place you at risk of type 2 diabetes, heart disease, weight gain, and even depression. At the very least, not sleeping enough is a way to feel miserable, tired, and cranky the next day. Making sure you get enough sleep is one thing you can do to take care of yourself and protect your mental and physical health.

If you aren't sure you're getting enough sleep, or you want to try to get more sleep (you can't sleep too much!), here are some things you might want to try to improve your sleep hygiene:

- Go to bed at the same time each night and wake up at the same time.
- Make sure your bed is comfortable to you.
- Make sure the room you sleep in is a comfortable temperature, not too hot or too cold.
- Don't eat a big meal too close to bedtime.

- Be careful not to drink anything with caffeine (such as soda or tea) in the afternoon or evening.
- Keep electronic devices out of your bedroom.
- Don't do other things in bed where you sleep.
- Don't study, watch television, or eat on your bed.

Don't sacrifice sleep for the screen

Speaking of electronic devices, if you're like a lot of kids these days, you have a parent who talks about **screen time** more that you would like them to. Your parent is probably in line with what the **American Academy of Pediatrics** (AAP, the biggest organization of doctors that focus on kids' health in the USA) recommends for kids' screen time, or as they put it, a "**healthy media diet.**" The AAP suggests that parents put limits on screen time and make sure their kids don't let screens interfere with sleep, physical activity, and health in general. They also suggest that parents make sure that kids experience media-free times with their families, such as dinner time. The AAP recommends that families sit down and talk about their media use and create a plan together.

Why am I talking about this in the chapter on physical activity? You've probably heard adults grumble that when they were kids they ran around outside and didn't spend all their time using a phone or a tablet. You've probably also heard about how kids these days are more likely to be overweight than in past generations. It turns out that the two things are linked. More screen time tends to mean less physical activity, which also tends to mean a greater likelihood of being overweight, and being overweight is associated with a variety of health risks. It's important to find some sort of balance. Watching television or videos and playing video games can be entertaining, but **taking good care of your body means making it move around most days.**

Q & A:

I know it's important to get enough sleep, but sometimes I just lie there at night thinking about everything that happened during the day. I worry about the next day. I start to worry about all sorts of things, and I can't sleep. What should I do?

It isn't uncommon for people to think about their days and even to worry a bit when they lie in bed at night. If you find yourself worrying a lot, then you may be experiencing anxiety that a professional could help you with. You may want to talk with a parent or other adult who you feel comfortable talking to, like an aunt or an older sibling. It may also be valuable to talk with a counselor at your school. Sometimes just talking about things that are on your mind can help a lot. Often, other people can help you understand that some of the things you're worried about are unlikely to happen or unlikely to matter very much in the grand scheme of things. This isn't to say that your worries are anything to be embarrassed about, just that getting other people's perspectives can be valuable.

In terms of getting more sleep, consider the tips above. You may want to try some relaxation exercises, or you could listen to relaxing music when you go to sleep. Sleeping well has a lot to do with forming good sleep habits and getting used to enjoying sleep, as opposed to feeling anxious in bed at night.

If talking with someone about your worries and adopting healthy sleep habits don't do the trick, then you may want to talk with a doctor. It's possible that you have a sleep disorder (although a true sleep disorder is fairly rare before adulthood, affecting just 4% of children, according to the Association of American Family Physicians), or that some medication may help you to cope with your anxiety (see also the discussion of anxiety in Chapter 9).

It's never too late

There's a chance that you're reading this and realizing that you aren't particularly interested in being more physically active than you already are, or that you just don't have the time, with school and other activities you're involved in. This is OK. We're all works in progress and we have the potential to become better in the future, whether that means becoming more knowledgeable about a particular topic, more involved in a certain hobby, or more engaged in physical activity.

Being a kid means juggling school, relationships with family and friends, and other extracurricular activities. If you don't want to or just can't find the time to do one more activity or responsibility right now, this isn't a reason to feel guilty. As you get older, you're likely to find more occasions and opportunities to engage in physical activity of all types. I became a runner in my mid-30s (nearly 10 years ago) after only a couple of years of running track as a kid. Running wasn't something I was that enthusiastic about or that committed to when I was younger. I can't even remember why I was on the track team for a few years—probably because I had some friends who did it so I did too. Now running is an important part of my life and it's something I've done a lot more of than I ever, ever expected I would when I was young. So even if you don't get into a particular form of exercise now, this doesn't mean that you won't when you're older. Most physical activity will benefit your mind and body, even if you don't make it a habit until you're an adult.

✓ **SUMMING UP #BEFIT**

☑ Being regularly physically active is an important part of taking care of your body and nurturing a positive body image.

☑ Physical activity can improve not just how you feel about yourself, but your mental and physical health as well. Being regularly active can even help you live a longer life.

☑ Don't sacrifice sleep to exercise, and be careful not to let screen time take the place of sleep or physical activity. It's important to find some balance so that you do things you enjoy (watch TV), things you have to do (homework), and things that are important for your health (physical activity and sleep). It can be difficult to achieve this balance, so be sure to ask friends or family for help establishing good habits.

FIND OUT MORE:

- The Centers for Disease Control and Prevention's website includes information about physical activity and sleep habits, such as www.cdc.gov/physicalactivity/index.html and www.cdc.gov/sleep/index.html.

- The American Academy of Pediatrics has an online worksheet that families can use to discuss the important issues around balancing media time, available at: www.healthychildren.org/English/media/Pages/default.aspx.

- For more scholarly articles and web pages with information about healthy eating and nutrition, see the companion website for this book: www.TheBodyImageBookforGirls.com.

CHAPTER 9

SELF-CARE

#BeMindful

> Respect your body.
> It's the only one you get.
>
> Anonymous

Nurturing a positive body image isn't only about feeling good about your appearance. It's about taking care of yourself—both your body and your mind. In this chapter, I discuss some strategies for self-care that you may want to adopt. I'll also review some things that may interfere with your ability to practice self-care so you can combat them and stay healthy for the rest of your life.

IN THIS CHAPTER, YOU'LL LEARN

○ how to be mindful about your physical and mental needs and to aim for positive embodiment,

○ how to identify when you may need extra self-care, such as if you experience anxiety, depression, or a chronic health condition, and

○ the importance of nurturing positive relationships with others who will support you on your journey to a positive body image.

What is mindfulness?

One way to care for yourself is to be mindful of your physical, psychological, social, and emotional needs. **Mindfulness** actually has two related definitions. To be mindful means to be aware. It's important to spend some time thinking about your needs; for example, you may find that you value some time alone each day. Or maybe you realize that you feel better when you get at least 8 hours of sleep each night.

Mindfulness also refers to being present in the moment, accepting your thoughts and feelings, and paying attention to yourself. There are different ways to try to achieve this sort of mindfulness, including yoga and **meditation**. A recent study provides some evidence for the usefulness of mindfulness in improving body image. In this study, young women were shown a series of brief videos about mindfulness, including videos about mindfulness in general, **breathing exercises**, and eating mindfully. At the end of the study, women's body image ratings showed some improvement, suggesting that learning about mindfulness was helpful.

Try yoga

Yoga has been popular with adults for a long time, but it's also becoming popular among children and teens. Yoga is a form of exercise, but can also be a good way to increase mindfulness. Through stretches, poses, and breathing exercises, yoga can help promote body awareness. Yoga can also encourage a focus on body functionality and acceptance. Because of all of this, researchers have begun to explore yoga practice as a way to improve body image.

Scientists have found that asking pre-teens to participate in a yoga program may increase their body appreciation. Among adults, practicing yoga has been shown to increase mindfulness and improve how people view themselves. Furthermore, practicing yoga may improve general body image. There is no guarantee that a weekly yoga class will dramatically alter how you feel about your body, but there is hardly any downside to trying yoga. You may improve your flexibility and strength, as well as your general well-being. Feeling better about your body could just be the icing on the cake.

Meditation is for everyone (maybe)

You've probably heard of **meditation** before, and you may have some basic idea of what it's all about. However, you may not realize that meditation is actually a broad term to describe a variety of techniques. All meditation techniques aim to train the mind, just as physical activity aims to train the body. Whereas physical activity is all about being active, meditation is about training the mind to be calm.

Meditation practices often involve breathing techniques to relax the body and calm the mind. Some forms of meditation involve stillness and focusing attention on a particular object while trying to clear thoughts from the mind. Meditation can also focus on acknowledging thoughts or concerns and working on accepting them or distancing yourself from them. Meditation includes listening to music that's enjoyable and soothing, and can even include reading or writing/journaling. The goal of any sort of meditation is to feel calm, relaxed, and "**centered**."

What does this have to do with body image? For some people, meditation can help them feel not only calmer, but also more in touch with their bodies. This sense of "being in touch with" or "happily living in" our bodies is sometimes referred to as **embodiment**. This may seem obvious, but we are our bodies. We cannot escape them. Feeling comfortable with, and accepting of, our bodies is an important part of developing a positive body image.

Some people enjoy meditation, but not everyone. You can get better at it with practice, but it also may not be for you. It typically involves stillness, reflection, and calmness. Some people don't like to be still, aren't particularly patient at reflecting on their experiences, and are naturally high-energy. These people may grow to like meditation, or it may not be a good fit for them. There are other ways to nurture your physical and emotional selves, so don't worry if meditation doesn't seem to be for you.

Other ways to relax

Typical mindfulness techniques are not for everyone. When I talked with a girl named Asiala in the process of writing this book, she mentioned that she'd gotten bored when she tried yoga and meditation. She felt fidgety and then also felt bad that she couldn't be calm and enjoy relaxing. I explained to Asiala that there is nothing wrong with feeling this way. It's possible that more practice with yoga or meditation may lead her to get more enjoyment out of these activities. It's also possible that these approaches to relaxation are never going to be relaxing to her. There are other ways to relax, feel in touch with yourself, and develop a positive body image.

I already discussed exercise in detail in Chapter 8, but exercise can be a great way to relax for some people. Of course, you have to be doing some sort of exercise that you enjoy in order for it to relax you. Or, at the very least, the exercise needs to tire you out and force you to relax. But even just short walks, enjoying the scenery around you and taking a break from the rest of your day, can be a good way to de-stress.

Relaxation practices are often described as activities that you must do alone. I don't think this is necessarily true. If I meet a friend for lunch and we talk, catch up and spend an hour or so just ignoring the stressors in our lives and enjoying each other's company, I feel relaxed afterwards. I'm sure I'm not the only one who finds socializing to be a source of relaxation at times, and talking with others a way to rethink things in your life that may be bothering you. Often, people we're close to can offer support and advice that makes us feel calmer and less frazzled by the demands of our lives. For some people, grooming and hygiene practices can be a source of relaxation. A long, warm shower or a hot bath can feel soothing and relaxing. Soaking in a bathtub of bubbly water and listening to some music you enjoy can be a nice way to unwind. Spending time washing your hair or cleaning your face can even be a way to feel like you're caring for yourself. After all, that's what self-care is: nurturing yourself in ways that you enjoy and make you feel good.

What if you feel like you need extra self-care?

There are a lot of great things about being a girl and a young woman, but there are also things that may feel challenging. The changes you experience physically as a result of puberty may feel strange and unsettling. Changes in your social world as you start a different school, participate in new activities, or make new friends can be exciting, but also stressful. It's also during adolescence that some mental health disorders tend to emerge (in other words, people may have a biological tendency to experience these disorders that doesn't become obvious until adolescence). Two relatively common mental disorders that you may experience are depression and anxiety. Fortunately, both of these disorders are treatable and there is a lot you can do to feel better if you experience either (or both) of these.

Depression

Depression is the most common psychological disorder. We all feel sad sometimes, but depression is more than just sadness. Usually, when a person experiences depression, she experiences physical, cognitive, and emotional symptoms. She may feel tired all the time or be unable to sleep. She may be hungry a lot or have no appetite at all, and may gain or lose weight. She may have a difficult time concentrating or completing tasks. She may also feel worthless and experience a sense of despair, as if life is not worth living.

Depression can be somewhat mild and last for a few months, or it may be severe and last for years. Sometimes life experiences, such as the loss of a loved one, can lead to depression, but it is believed there is also a biological and genetic component to depression. Regardless of what leads someone to experience depression, it isn't their fault. No one wants to feel sad and hopeless, and anyone who does should consider seeking advice from a doctor

MYTHS AND MISBELIEFS

Vitamins and other natural supplements are the best and safest way to treat depression.

If you're concerned that you or someone you care about needs treatment for depression, the first step is probably for the depressed person to talk with a therapist. There are no downsides to talking with someone who can offer support, ways to rethink issues that may contribute to depression, and strategies for coping.

There are many types of therapists. Some may offer free services at your school or in a local clinic. Some may see patients in a private practice and typically charge by the hour. Some therapists are trained to help people cope specifically with depression (versus other mental health issues). Some are trained specifically to help children and adolescents. It can be important for patients to find someone to talk with who suits their needs, in terms of where they provide treatment, what their fees may be, and their ability to help people cope with depression in particular.

Some people who experience depression may benefit from antidepressant medications. The most popular of these is probably Prozac, although there are many different kinds of antidepressants (most of which have been created more recently than Prozac). **Antidepressant medication** can be truly life-saving for some people. However, these medications do sometimes come with side-effects that are undesirable, such as drowsiness, a dry mouth, and even nausea.

Some people prefer not to take medications unless absolutely necessary. They may seek out a different sort of remedy, such as vitamins. While there is not a lot of scientific evidence to suggest that vitamins will help someone cope with depression, according to the Mayo Clinic (a prestigious medical organization in the USA), vitamin B12 and other B vitamins may alter brain chemistry in such a way as to affect mood. Vitamin D has also received some attention as possibly being associated with mood.

However, here's something interesting that you probably didn't know: vitamins and **natural supplements** are not regulated by the Food and Drug Administration in the USA (although they are in the UK). What does that mean? Well, it means that, unlike other medicine, there are no quality checks on what contributes to the creation of vitamins and supplements in the USA. So there may be risks associated with vitamins and supplements, as well. And in the case of vitamin D, most people get what they need just from sunlight.

or counselor—especially if the symptoms of depression last for more than a few weeks.

There are different treatments for depression, and often a combination of treatments works the best. Talking with a therapist can be an important part of treatment for depression (see earlier Myths and Misbeliefs). Antidepressant medication can also be helpful. If you think you're depressed, be sure to talk with an adult who you trust about finding some treatment. There are some things you can do on your own—talk with friends, exercise, participate in activities you enjoy—that may make you feel better, but don't try to tackle depression on your own.

Anxiety

Most likely, you have felt anxious at least once in your life. Maybe you've had to give a presentation at school and you felt yourself start to sweat a bit or felt your heart start to race. This is a normal emotional response to a stressful situation. However, if you feel anxious a lot of the time, then you may have an **anxiety disorder**. There are different types of anxiety disorders, but they to tend affect people's ability to concentrate and focus, and often lead people to avoid certain situations. Anxiety can also affect sleep patterns (for example, making it difficult to sleep) and eating habits (leading people to eat more or less than they usually do). People who have anxiety disorders usually experience symptoms nearly every day for six months or more, and have a hard time keeping up with their daily routines at home, work, or school.

Anxiety can be very difficult to deal with, but it's treatable. Talking with a therapist can be a good first step toward coping with anxiety. A therapist can help you think through what's making you anxious and help you change habits and behaviors that may contribute to your anxiety. **Anti-anxiety medication** may also prove helpful. Similar to antidepressant medication, anti-anxiety medication alters the chemicals in a person's brain and can make a person feel calmer and happier. Stress management techniques, such as yoga and other approaches to mindfulness, can also help to reduce anxiety. But many people need more than mindfulness to cope with anxiety.

Q & A:

It feels like whenever adults talk about social media, they're negative and assume that social media is going to make us depressed or dissatisfied with our bodies. Can't social media be a good part of teenagers' lives?

Adults have a lot of concerns about how social media affects young people, probably partially because they did not grow up with it and they don't tend to understand it as well as young people do. Not all of adults' concerns are justified. In fact, there is some scientific evidence to suggest that social media can be a source of support for teens.

For example, although some research suggests that connecting with peers on social media may not always be a positive experience, connecting with family may be. This may be because young people are more likely to compare themselves to other kids their age, but don't make these comparisons with their family. Also, a new study suggests that body-positive posts on social media (sometimes called #BoPo) may improve young women's body satisfaction and overall mood. Perhaps one way to make your use of social media a good experience is to be thoughtful about who you connect with, and do your best to keep it positive.

(Note: if you're dealing with a serious health issue such as an eating disorder or depression, be sure that you don't rely on the internet or social media as your main source of support. You need a trained professional to help you.)

Other reasons for extra self-care

Some people need extra self-care, not because of their mental health, but because of a physical health condition or disability. In fact, by adulthood, more than half of all people experience some type of chronic health condition. These conditions may be somewhat minor, such as seasonal allergies, or they may be more complicated and serious, such as diabetes or heart disease. Most of these conditions require some extra self-care in order for people to function optimally.

It can be very difficult to maintain the sort of health regimen that may be required if you have (or develop) a chronic condition or disability. Your doctor is likely to prescribe medicine that may be helpful. You may have more doctor appointments. You may need to make changes to your lifestyle, including changes to what you eat or what sort of exercise you do. It would also be normal to feel somewhat let down by your body, or to wish that you didn't have to deal with these things.

In recent research looking at body image among people who experience chronic pain, individuals who are more accepting of their pain tend to have more positive body images. It seems that health problems don't have to lead people to view their bodies negatively. It really matters how people think about their health. If they're accepting of their health problems—after all, most people will have some kind of health problem at some point and understand that they need to cope with it—it's less disruptive to their feelings about their body overall. This isn't to say that you should feel glad about having to deal with a health problem. But if you do experience a health problem or disability, there are things you can do to help yourself cope. Never feel like you need to deal with this sort of thing alone. Support from caring others can be important if you find yourself in need of an extra dose of self-care.

MY STORY

Emma Renne, 20 years old

It has taken me a long time to accept my body for what it is. However, going to college has really helped change my level of confidence in myself. I started stepping outside of my comfort zone all around, including wearing clothes I would have never typically worn in high school. I remember the first time I wore a tube top to a party. I would have never worn a tube top in high school, especially not without a bra. For a girl who wears a 36D bra, sometimes you're told, "Oh you can't wear that, your boobs are too big." For me, my boobs were not the hardest part of wearing a tube top, it was my stomach. Even in high-waisted jeans I was still concerned about how my stomach looked. It wasn't just about my stomach being fat, it was about the continuous glucose monitor I wear on my stomach for my diabetes that clearly sticks out like a sore thumb when I'm out. Sometimes I'll get lucky and I'll have placed it in a good enough spot that my jeans will come up high enough to cover it, but sometimes it still shows. It took me a while to be completely comfortable with wearing my glucose monitor on my stomach because I always worried about looking like a complete robot. I also wear an insulin pump on my arm that is completely noticeable 90% of the time, so I did not want to have to wear anything else to make me stand out even more. But after a while of being on campus and seeing girls wear what they wanted to confidently, I decided to give it a try myself. One day I went out and started buying different clothes that I would not have worn before. Now my closet is full of super-cute clothes that make me look and feel good.

My mom has always been my biggest supporter and very best friend. I think for her it all goes back to her own insecurities and making sure I never feel about myself the way she did about herself. Every day my mom finds some way to remind me how beautiful I am, even if I look like I have just crawled out from under a rock. To take it a step further, when I am feeling down on my body specifically, she tells me that my body is beautiful. She doesn't push me to do anything differently, she doesn't talk down to me or ever minimize how I'm feeling; she just supports me. Sometimes when I am wearing an outfit that looks really good on me she'll ask me if people threw rose petals down on the ground for me when I walked in the room. I just laugh and tell her, "No." There are other times where she'll think an outfit looks really good on me and then ask me if anyone else has told me how beautiful I was today. Again, I just laugh. It's so cute how she thinks that everyone I will ever meet will think I am as beautiful as she thinks I am. But even if no one else besides her thinks that, that's all I need.

Being a girl is hard enough without having body image insecurities. I think it's really important to teach young girls to be nice to each other—and nice to themselves. It's our responsibility to be kind to one another. It doesn't need to be a competition with each other about who is more successful than the other. Instead, share your successes and accomplishments with other girls. Make your confidence your favorite accessory each day. Wear your beauty with pride and a big smile and hold your head up high. When I feel a little down on myself, I remember my favorite quote, "Confidence looks good on you, girl!"

Girl power

When I interviewed girls in the process of writing this book, one thing that came up over and over again was the importance of friends. Nearly everyone agreed that you don't need a dozen or two dozen friends, or hundreds of followers on Instagram. One or two good friends goes a long way. **Girls can do anything! But they can't necessarily do it on their own. Everyone needs support, help, and love from others.**

Friends can be an important part of growing up and developing body positivity for a variety of reasons. Feeling good about yourself, body and mind, can be easier when you feel that others feel good about you too. This isn't to say that you let other people determine your sense of yourself, just that we all find it helpful to feel supported by other people.

It's possible that you don't feel like you have a lot of close friends, and that's OK. It may be that you don't feel like you fit in well at your school, or that other kids don't share your interests. There are many successful adults who describe themselves as loners during their childhood. Both Bill Gates (the co-founder of Microsoft and one of the wealthiest people in the world) and Steve Jobs (the deceased co-founder of Apple) are described as "nerds" who didn't fit in with their classmates when they were growing up. Like them, you may find enjoyment in developing a particular skill or hobby, and you may eventually meet more people who share your interests. Even if you don't feel like you have close friends now, this doesn't mean that you won't develop important friendships later, or that you shouldn't try to connect with people you enjoy spending time with.

Your family may be a valuable source of support, especially if you feel that your friendships are lacking in any way. However, it's totally normal for you to prefer the company of friends your own age to parents or other family members. It's also typical for teens to feel like their parents, in particular, don't understand what their life is like at school and with kids their age. To a certain extent, this is probably true. But in most cases, your family wants what is best for you, and they want you to grow up to be happy and healthy. Even if it doesn't feel like they "get you," they're usually happy to talk with you and offer whatever support they can. Sometimes you just have to give them a chance.

Some people don't have close family relationships, and for a variety of reasons may not develop a lot of close friendships in their childhood and adolescence. However, there are a lot of other people who care about you and can be a friend to you. Maybe there is a teacher or a coach you admire, and who seems invested in you. It's OK to turn to that person for advice. They probably chose that career because they enjoy hanging out with kids and want to be helpful to people like you. There is good evidence that adult mentors (trusted adult advisors) can have very positive effects on young people's lives. I know that when my students have asked me for advice, I always do my best to be helpful and I feel flattered that they want my advice. In other words, you're probably not going to burden a teacher, coach, or other adult in your life if you turn to them for advice or support. Remember, they were once kids too.

Q & A:

It sometimes feels like the most popular girls at school aren't all that nice. It seems like they're only popular because they look a certain way. But a part of me still wants to be accepted by these girls and be popular too. Does everyone just want to be popular?

In the process of writing this book, I talked with more than one girl who had a question like this. The way one girl I interviewed, Mary, put it, "Why can't everyone just be nice?"

It can be difficult to think through these issues as you grow up—and even when you're an adult. Most of us want to be liked by others, and even to be popular. But most of us may not feel that we're always accepted. As the saying goes, you can't please all of the people all of the time.

One way to think about acceptance is to think about the people you can just be yourself around. If you feel like you don't have to work to impress certain people, then those people are probably your true friends. Maybe you haven't found those people yet? Look for them! In other words, find your "tribe" of people who share your interests, or sense of humor, or goals in life. Instead of trying to fit in, find out where you belong.

And what about the people who may not always seem nice? Perhaps the best strategy is to ignore them. When you cross paths with people who aren't your favorites, try to be nice to them anyway. You may not realize exactly what's going on in their lives, and maybe they're struggling in their own way. If they aren't being nice to you, they may be feeling insecure or jealous, they may be experiencing problems at home, or they may be looking for attention. Remember that people are complicated, and their behavior is influenced by many factors; how someone treats you may actually have very little to do with you.

Sharing the love

At some point during your adolescence, you're likely to want to form a romantic relationship with a boy or a girl. Of course, you'll say that you're "hanging out," or that you "like" or that you're "with" this person. Maybe this relationship will turn serious, maybe it won't. Maybe there will be many of them while you're a teenager, maybe there won't be any until you're an adult. Why am I talking about this in a book about body image? Because all of our relationships impact us in different ways. Body image isn't just about how we look, but about how we feel about ourselves. Our relationships can play a role in all of this.

The start of a romantic relationship of any kind can affect how you think about yourself and may challenge who you are. You may feel like you should try to be someone different to be liked by someone you're interested in, or who is your boyfriend/girlfriend. There is also scientific evidence to suggest that boys and men care more about how their girlfriends look than girls and women care about how their boyfriends look. (You may not have needed me to tell you this.) If you feel like you're concerned about your appearance due to your interest in another person, this may be fairly normal. However—and this is important—you should never feel like you need to look or be someone different to attract someone else's interest. **A significant other *should* be a source of support and love and only add to your positive sense of yourself.** In fact, there is research to suggest that people who are in serious relationships typically feel better about their body image than people who are not.

Q & A:

All my friends have started dating, but I haven't had a boyfriend yet. How do I get a boyfriend?

It's normal to want to do what your friends are doing, and it's normal to be thinking about forming romantic relationships during your teens. However, dating is not an accomplishment. It's probably not ideal to think of a boyfriend (or girlfriend) as something to "go after."

As I mentioned above, our relationships can influence how we feel about ourselves. Having a boyfriend or girlfriend may make you feel attractive, appreciated, or even loved. But you shouldn't need to rely on others to feel those things about yourself.

Taking care of yourself means being true to yourself and not changing who you are to gain the approval of anyone else. Some people develop romantic relationships for the first time when they're young, and some people don't until adulthood. In order for any relationship to bring you long-term happiness, you need to be sure that it doesn't interfere with your self-care.

Q & A:

Sometimes it feels like you can't win when you're a girl. Girls who get a lot of attention from boys are called "easy," "fast," or "hoes." But not getting any attention can feel lonely. Why is this?

This is a great question, and I wish I had a good answer. But I think you're right, that it can often feel like a no-win for girls. It's unfortunate that girls are sometimes held responsible for how other people perceive them, even though others' perceptions are their own problems.

It's important to know yourself and to take care of yourself. It's important that other people's perceptions of you don't shape how you feel about yourself. It's OK to want positive attention from others, but not to want to be whistled at by a man your father's age. And it's really important that you talk to an adult you trust if you're getting attention that feels wrong or makes you uncomfortable.

You should not feel powerless. Women and girls are half of all the people on the planet. They can—and in many ways have been doing so for decades—demand more respect from and equality with boys and men. It's important that you are a part of making things better for all girls and women in whatever way you can.

A final thought about self-care

Taking good care of yourself and nurturing your body image will take some time and energy. It's OK to think of this as a priority in your life, and not to feel guilty for spending this time on yourself. Girls and women often find themselves in the position of caring for others, including younger siblings, cousins, and even their significant others. **In order to be helpful to others, you need to take care of yourself first. And you should expect that other people who care about you will support your efforts at self-care and the development of a positive body image.**

✓ SUMMING UP #BEMINDFUL

✓ Developing your positive body image means taking care of yourself—body and mind. One way to do this is to practice mindfulness techniques like yoga or meditation.

✓ If you feel that you need extra support as you try to care for yourself, be sure to talk with a counselor, therapist, doctor, or other adult who can offer that support or can find helpful resources.

✓ Nurturing your relationships with other people is an important part of self-care. But it may also be important to avoid people who are not positive influences on your positive body image and well-being.

FIND OUT MORE:

- There is a chapter by Catherine Cook-Cottone about self-care and body image in the book I edited with colleagues Elizabeth Daniels and Meghan Gillen: *Body Positive: Understanding and Improving Body Image in Science and Practice* (2018). Publisher: Cambridge University Press.

- For information about therapists that may be of help in treating depression or anxiety, see the **American Psychological Association**'s web page available at: www.apa.org/topics/depression/index, or the **British Psychological Society**'s website, available at: www.bps.org.uk/

- For more scholarly articles and web pages with information about healthy eating and nutrition, see the companion website for this book: www.TheBodyImageBookforGirls.com.

CHAPTER 10

BE THE CHANGE

#BeBodyPositive

> Be the change that you wish to see in the world.
>
> Mahatma Gandhi, Indian lawyer, politician, social activist

You and your body are inseparable; your body is the place where you "live." **Taking care of your body, accepting it, and protecting your health are all important parts of developing a positive body image.** Our culture tends to emphasize the importance of women's appearances, making it easy for girls and women to doubt themselves and experience body dissatisfaction. Hopefully, after reading this far, you understand that you can choose to have a positive body image, even though it may require a bit of work on your part.

Nurturing a positive body image is important because your body image affects many other aspects of your mental and physical health. It's also important because, by exhibiting a positive body image, you have the power to start to change how other girls think about their bodies. If you think and talk about your body differently from how girls and women typically do (which, unfortunately, is usually negatively), you can help promote positive change. Or, in the words of Gandhi, you can "be the change."

It's not always easy to do things differently from most other people. So in this chapter I want to leave you with some reminders of why this is so important, some potential obstacles on your personal journey, and some things to think about when you feel discouraged.

> ⤷ **IN THIS CHAPTER, YOU'LL LEARN**
>
> ○ the importance of being kind and accepting of yourself and others, and not falling for other people's narrow ideas about what is beautiful or how you should look,
> ○ how focusing on meaningful issues outside of yourself can contribute to your positive sense of yourself, and
> ○ that you can play a part in helping others develop positive body images.

Remember: You are your own worst critic

We can be harder on ourselves than we ever are on anyone else. We feel bad about ourselves for not looking a certain way and then we feel bad for caring that we don't look a certain way. Then we can feel even worse for spending time and energy on any of these worries.

If you feel like you're down on yourself, take a step back and try to quiet these negative thoughts. Remember the importance of self-compassion and self-acceptance. Both of these attitudes will do a lot more for you than self-hate ever will. No one is perfect by everyone's standards, so you can stop aiming for perfect. You can be upset about this, or you can work toward treating yourself with kindness and acceptance.

Don't compare or despair

It's natural for us to compare ourselves with other people, but this tendency to compare ourselves with others, or social comparison, can be problematic. We're all unique in our own ways, and trying to be like someone else will rarely work. Changing our looks (or our personalities, for that matter) is harder than it appears. Most of our qualities have a strong biological component that makes them only partially changeable. We can get cosmetic surgery and change our nose, but it's nearly impossible to get longer legs, narrower hips, or a different sense of humor.

The science examining social comparison is pretty convincing, too. Most recently, researchers have examined how comparing ourselves with others on social media can be a negative experience, but

MY STORY

April Meyers, 14 years old

I've been on the skinnier side my whole life, so in a way I guess I'm lucky. I've never felt "fat." However, I've always felt too skinny, and that my "stick arms and legs" were awkward and ugly. This makes me super self-conscious in bathing suits and tank tops. I've also always felt that my stomach "wasn't flat enough" and that I had too large a stomach. I can find something wrong with every part of my body.

Over time I've realized that hating yourself shouldn't be the default. Although that's what's portrayed as normal in the media, it's not healthy. Everyone should love themselves, no matter what. Even when I'm still uncomfortable with the way I look, I try to have this mindset, and then I feel better.

Something that has helped me understand I'm not as awkward and ugly as I feel is comparing myself to others. Not in a "look at that girl, I'm prettier than her" way, because that's wrong and you should never, ever bring down other girls. But I find myself thinking, "Look, you think she's beautiful and she looks very similar to you, so why don't you think the same about yourself?" That has helped me realize that I'm just as beautiful as I think every other girl is.

I've thought a lot about how to talk with other girls about body issues: don't comment on their body—period. A good rule to live by is: If they can't change it within five minutes, don't mention it. That means that you can let your friend know they have something on their face or shirt, but you cannot tell them that "they are too fat." Even if you think something is neutral or a compliment, still don't say it. You never know when you could hurt someone's feelings, and being a good friend is all about being supportive.

Sometimes I think your mind can be your worst enemy, and no one actually thinks about how you look except for yourself. Once you conquer the voices in your head, and convince them you're beautiful, no one can stop you.

doesn't have to be. It turns out that not everyone who sees something positive on others' social media newsfeed is then discouraged about their own lives. The key seems to be to focus on the emotional message in posts, not the content so much. People who see positive things ("Look at how happy she looks") and think about the positive emotions shown ("It's great to see someone looking happy") have a more positive experience using social media. They actual report an improvement in their own mood. The trick is not to take it that one step further and think, "She looks so happy and I'm not that happy—what's wrong with me?" In other words, comparing is what leads to despairing, so don't go there.

Q & A:

I don't want to care about material things like clothes and make-up, but I do. How do I change the way I think about these things?

It's important to realize that many—perhaps, most—people care about material items. How we present ourselves to the world, with the clothes we wear and the other ways that we try to look nice, matters to most people. Don't feel bad for wanting to look nice, or for caring about material things.

But remember that these material things are unlikely to bring you lasting happiness. A new pair of designer jeans may make you feel good for a few weeks or months, but they're unlikely to make you feel all that special years later. A stylish haircut may grant you some attention for days or weeks, but then you'll get used to it and your hair will grow out.

We're all bombarded with so many advertisements for material goods and beauty products that it's easy to feel like there is something wrong with us and that we need to "fix" ourselves by dressing a certain way or using certain cosmetics. It can seem like success in life is all about having certain things. But all of these things can only change us temporarily and in superficial ways. It's important, but sometimes very difficult, to keep this in perspective and to realize that who we are—what makes us a caring person, a valued friend, and a decent human being—has very little to do with material things.

Don't get beauty sick

Beauty sickness has been described by psychologist Renee Engeln as what happens when women spend energy worrying about their appearance at the cost of focusing on things like their education, careers, family, relationships, and even their communities. It's not that there is anything wrong with wanting to be beautiful. Who doesn't want to be beautiful? The problem is wanting it more than anything else.

It's easy to notice that very attractive people often get more attention from others and may even be treated better than others. However, there is a serious downside to being valued for your appearance. For one thing, maintaining beauty often requires a lot of work. It's hard to be engaged with the world and enjoying your life if you're constantly worried about how you look. You can choose to care less about how you compare with beauty ideals. You can think of your body more in terms of its functionality. You can remember that it's your body that allows you to move, be in, and experience the world. It's what allows you to do so much—it's *not* what's holding you back.

Don't stigmatize

Another problem with our cultural focus on beauty is that it's usually all about one (or a few) particular look(s). It's rarely about diversity and inclusion—accepting everyone as they are. Very few people can fit into the exact "looks" deemed beautiful by our culture, because we all come in different shapes and sizes. Most of us aren't light skinned, long legged, and blond. We have different colored skin, hair, and eyes. We have different sized noses, ears, and breasts. Defining beauty more broadly, to include some of these variations, is an important way to appreciate one another and work toward accepting ourselves.

Unfortunately, there is often far more cultural focus on **stigmatizing** people who don't fit **society**'s views of beauty than in accepting people who look different. Stigma is probably a word you've heard before, but maybe you aren't sure exactly what it means. People can be stigmatized or feel stigma for a variety of qualities they may possess: their race, gender, disability status, or weight are some of the most common qualities that may lead to stigma. If someone is stigmatized, they are mistreated because of these qualities and are often assumed to have negative characteristics associated with these qualities. **Weight stigma** (also referred to as **weight bias** and **weight-based discrimination**) occurs when a person is mistreated because she is overweight. (It's also possible to experience stigma for being underweight, but this happens much less often.) The person may also be assumed to be lazy or addicted to junk food, just because she has a larger body.

MY STORY

Cecile Asia, 23 years old

When thinking about body image, I can say with confidence that I don't hate my body. However, I do struggle with accepting it completely. I find myself thinking about the things that frustrate me regarding my body and the things I want to change. I try to combat these thoughts by reminding myself that my body is a part of me and I'm just thankful to have one that works. I don't know that I've ever thought to myself, "I love my body," but I am able to stop myself from having recurring negative thoughts about it.

I probably think more about how my body functions because when I was 12, I was diagnosed with **hyperthyroidism** and **Graves' disease** (an **autoimmune disorder**). My body was producing too much thyroid hormone and I had an extremely overactive metabolism, among other symptoms. My doctor had me try multiple medications, but I was allergic to one and the other didn't work, so I had to cease physical activity due to my abnormally fast heart rate (another symptom). But then I got pneumonia so we had to take almost immediate action. I was given a radioactive iodine treatment which basically renders my thyroid inactive, giving me **hypothyroidism** instead. As this is the exact opposite of hyperthyroidism, I started to gain weight due to a slower metabolism.

I was finally a healthy weight for my height and build, but to me it was pretty off-putting. I, like many others, subconsciously equated being

Weight stigma is incredibly problematic, not just because it's unfair to mistreat anyone based on how they look, but because it's associated with other problems. When a person experiences stigma, they often start to believe others' negative views of them. Experiencing weight stigma has also been associated with the development of body dissatisfaction, eating disorders, and depression. Unfortunately, the rates of weight stigma have risen dramatically in recent years. In fact, some scientists who study weight stigma have referred to it as the last acceptable form of discrimination. What they mean by this is that people often feel that it's acceptable to mistreat larger people because their body size is their fault. Hopefully, after reading this book, you understand that weight is a much more complicated issue, and our size has a lot to do with our biology. **Furthermore, blaming or mistreating people for anything is rarely a helpful way to interact with them. Just as self-compassion is incredibly important, compassion for others is essential too.**

skinny with being attractive and happy, and being fat with being ugly and miserable. I think my mom is a large part of why I made it through this period of my life without too many issues. She would remind me of how healthy I looked and how scared she was for me when I had hyperthyroidism. At some point, I stopped thinking of my skinnier self as a better version of me because I was not healthy when I was skinny.

Another positive influence on my body image was actually going to a women's college for two years. Because body image issues are so prevalent among women, there was a big push to reinforce positive body image at Smith College. We learned how to implement positive affirmations regarding body image. We also made it a point not to comment about what others were eating and instead think about how food was meant to nourish and be enjoyed.

My advice for younger girls would be to be thankful for the body they have. It's important to remind yourself of all the work your body does each day that allows you to experience life. And don't look at the number on the scale—your health and self-worth isn't determined by a number. Instead, focus on how you feel, and if your doctor says your body is functioning properly, then you're good to go. I also think that it's normal to want to change things about your body, but this isn't going to make you happier or increase your worth as a person. It's important to separate the appearance of our bodies from achieving happiness.

Understand that our food environment probably isn't helping

In most modern societies, people have plenty of food available and a lot of that food is unhealthy. Corner stores, vending machines, and drive-through restaurants all make it easy to get food when you're hungry, but hard to make healthy choices. Although fruits and vegetables are sometimes sold at convenience stores and stands, you're more likely to find very appetizing, fairly unhealthy options. If you go out to eat at a restaurant, the portions are likely to be bigger than any one person requires.

Taking care of your body means feeding it well. True body positivity includes healthy food choices most of the time. But when an unhealthy option is around every corner, it can feel like an ongoing internal struggle. Don't feel like you need to restrict yourself from foods you enjoy, but you shouldn't get lunch from a vending machine or drive-through every day either.

Our food environment can feel overwhelming and outside of our control. It may be difficult for us to change the general food environment around us, but we can work toward having a healthy, personal food environment in our homes. Asking our families about keeping healthy snacks that we enjoy on hand and trying to have healthy meals (most of the time) can be an important way to be sure that our bodies get the nutrients they need. It's also important to try new foods, and to give those foods a chance. Sometimes when we try new foods, we don't like them, but if we try them more than once we may actually grow to like them. Psychologists who study food have actually found that most people need to try a food as many as eight times before they develop a liking for it. If you don't like kale the first time you try it, you may need to give it another chance (or seven more chances). Being aware of our food options and choices, without worrying about them, can be a responsible way to focus on staying healthy.

Try to think outside yourself

In research that aims to understand why some people have more positive body images than others, scientists have found that focusing outside yourself can be good for how you feel about yourself. In this research, people who engaged with projects or causes that they thought were important, including focusing on school work or volunteering at an animal shelter, spent less energy concerned with their own bodies. It seems that thinking about issues bigger than oneself may be important for keeping some perspective.

It makes sense, right? There are only so many hours in the day, and if you fill those hours with work or causes that are meaningful to you, there will be less time to worry about whether or not you're wearing the most stylish new brand of jeans. And you may feel less inclined to care!

Q & A:

What's one easy thing we can all do to help improve other young girls' body images?

Part of what leads girls to develop body image concerns is feeling that how they look is incredibly important. Our culture gives girls this idea in a variety of ways, through advertising, music, movies, and social media. What if we all tried to talk with girls less about their appearance and focused more on other things?

It seems to come to us naturally to compliment our friends and other girls on their appearance, whether it's their hair, clothes, or make-up. In some ways, this is how girls and women connect with each other—and who doesn't like compliments? But we could all get a bit better about starting conversations about other topics. We could talk about books we're reading, things we've done recently, hobbies, and our goals and aspirations. If we value girls for their brains over their bodies more often, their focus will be different as well.

Reasons for hope

Although media and celebrity culture—never mind our current food environment—aren't particularly helpful in the development of positive body images, there are some reasons to hope that change is on the way. Some advertisers have begun to promote their products using body-positive messages. For example, Dove (a company that makes soap and other cleansing and beauty products) has created a variety of advertisements in print and video that feature models of diverse body shapes, sizes, and ethnic backgrounds. Aerie, an underwear and clothing company, has a similar advertising campaign, which they call "Aerie Real." Aerie Real only uses images of women that have not been modified using Photoshop or other software. There is some research to suggest that these more "real" images are better for women's body images than images of super-slender, super-perfected, unattainable models. Hopefully, women's positive responses to these sorts of campaigns will lead to the use of more "real" women in advertising.

In addition to these advertising campaigns, there are other reasons for hope. Some celebrities have begun to demand that the media represent them accurately by using unedited photos. Lady Gaga, Kiera Knightley, Serena Williams, Jamie Lee Curtis, Lorde, Kate Winslet, Ashley Benson, and Colbie Caillat are among the women who have asked that pictures of themselves *not* be photoshopped. They want others to know that, even though they are famous, they are not perfect, and that is OK. There are also body-positive influencers on social media. There are podcasts about body positivity and rejecting diet culture. And there are web pages that contain helpful resources for people looking to improve their body image. Not everyone knows about all of these resources, but hopefully that will change with time and they will inspire more and more people.

☆ MYTHS AND MISBELIEFS

I've heard about celebrities like Beyoncé and Gwyneth Paltrow trying out diets like the "Herculean" diet and detox diets to look a certain way for certain events and performances. These things seem to work for them, but you warned against all diets in Chapter 6. If it's good for Beyoncé and Gwyneth, it must be good for me too.

Drastic diets can lead people to lose weight, and they may lose weight relatively fast. The biggest problem with any diet that dramatically alters someone's eating habits and is extremely restrictive is that it's unlikely to be something they can stick with. Once a person's eating habits return to what they were before the drastic diet, the weight will come back fast. In fact, research makes it pretty clear that people are likely to gain more weight than they originally lost.

There are other risks associated with drastic diets, including negative effects on your metabolism. When people lose weight, then gain weight, then lose weight again (sometimes referred to as **yo-yo dieting** because of the way a toy yo-yo bounces up and down) their metabolism is likely to slow, making it harder to maintain a lower weight. Drastic dieting habits have also been shown to contribute to the development of eating disorders, which can be extremely serious and life-threatening (look back to Chapter 7 for more information on eating disorders).

The bottom line is that drastic, celebrity-endorsed diets aren't a healthy approach to eating, and are likely to cause more harm than good in the long run.

Positive Body Image Resources

Body Positivity: www.youtube.com/channel/UC5ByY8fYOn0REFHARFGiJfA	YouTube channel containing short positive body image lessons
UConn Rudd Center for Food Policy and Obesity: www.uconnruddcenter.org	Internationally known center that studies and promotes health and reduction in weight bias
Hi.ur.beautiful: www.instagram.com/hi.ur.beautiful	Body positivity Instagram influencer
Mirna Valerio, known as Fat Girl Running: http://fatgirlrunning-fatrunner.blogspot.com, www.womensrunning.com/category/fat-girl-running	Body positivity blog about being active no matter your body size
Megan Jayne Crabbe, known as BodyPosiPanda: www.instagram.com/bodyposipanda/?hl=en	Body positivity Instagram influencer
Big Things with Zach Micho: https://bigthingspod.com/episodes	Plus-size model and body positivity Instagram influencer
Mama Cax: https://mamacax.com	Model, body positivity Instagram influencer, disability advocate, blogger
The Full Bloom Project: www.FullBloomProject.com	Podcast and web page with resources for improving body image
Rosie Beeme: www.instagram.com/roseybeeme/	Instagram influencer, body positivity blogger
Jes Baker: www.themilitantbaker.com	Body positivity blogger, author
Mind Your Body: www.psychologytoday.com/us/blog/mind-your-body	Blog containing evidence-based positive body image articles and discussions of gender

Continues on next page ...

National Eating Disorders Association (NEDA): www.NationalEatingDisorders.org	Largest non-profit organization dedicated to supporting individuals and families affected by eating disorders; serves as a catalyst for prevention, cures and access to quality care
Katie Sturino: www.instagram.com/katiesturino/	Body positivity Instagram influencer
Beauty Sick: www.psychologytoday.com/us/experts/renee-engeln-phd	Blog containing evidence-based positive body image messages and comments on "beauty culture"
I weigh: @i_weigh, www.iweighcommunity.com	Web page, body positivity and inclusivity advocates
Smart People Don't Diet: www.psychologytoday.com/us/blog/smart-people-don-t-diet	Blog containing evidence-based articles that are anti-diet and all about body image

Be the change

Cultural change can be slow. The things that people in any society value and expect from each other—to look or act a certain way—doesn't change overnight. But cultural change is possible. In fact, people have not always valued thinness or the fashions that we value today. If you look at pictures depicting people from a few

hundred years ago, men wore their hair in long ponytails (think George Washington) and even wore white, long-haired wigs, and women wore corsets to make their waists smaller and their hips appear relatively wider. Just over 100 years ago, women only wore skirts and dresses and men always wore top hats when they left the house. Even 20 years ago, most white women aimed to have small rear-ends, and now butt enhancements are trending.

There will always be trends in terms of what our culture suggests we do to make our bodies look attractive. Some of the trends may be relatively harmless (for example, certain hairstyles), but some may be relatively risky (for example, some forms of cosmetic surgery). We don't have to agree with these trends or follow them. When something seems unhealthy or even just uncomfortable, we can go our own way. If we reject certain trends, others may feel empowered to as well. If consumers don't buy certain products, companies will stop producing them. If we stop following certain influencers on Instagram, they may become less popular and less powerful.

As individuals we can contribute to cultural change. We can work to improve our own positive body images and we can become part of a movement where more and more girls and women do as well. **We can do our part to create a world where it is normal for girls and women to appreciate their bodies and not be dissatisfied with them.**

What exactly would that world look like?

Why don't we try to find out?

SUMMING UP #BEBODYPOSITIVE

✓ There are many reasons why it's important to develop a positive body image, one of which is that by exhibiting a positive body image you have the power to start to change how other girls think about their bodies.

✓ Current beauty ideals and the cultural focus on our appearance can make it difficult to feel good about your body, but it's important that you don't fall prey to beauty sickness, or stigmatize those who have larger bodies.

✓ Thinking about issues that are more important than how you look, and being engaged with issues that are meaningful to you, can help you develop as a well-rounded, confident person. By choosing to foster your positive body image you set an example for those around you and help to lead your society closer to understanding how important it is for all of us to be accepting and positive about who we are.

GLOSSARY

Acceptance (*also see self-acceptance*): Approving of something without wanting to change anything about it.

Acne (pimples, spots; breaking out): A skin condition where pores become clogged with oil, bacteria and dead skin cells; results in an inflamed eruption of the skin.

Active: Sporty, energetic, or physically engaged.

Activists (activism): People who participate in, get involved in, campaign for, or bring awareness to, a certain situation and act on it to make a change.

Adaptive appearance investment: Regularly engaging in appearance-related self-care, such as grooming behaviors that protect an individual's sense of style and personality. Usually includes enhancing one's natural features via non-harmful methods.

Adolescence: The stage of physical and mental development that occurs between childhood and adulthood; this stage is often marked by the onset of puberty.

Advertising (advertisement): A form of communication that markets or promotes a message in order to sell something.

American Academy of Pediatrics: A large organization of doctors in the USA that focuses on kids' health.

American Psychological Association: The largest professional organization for psychologists in the USA; their main goal is to further grow and develop the field of psychology.

American Society of Plastic Surgeons: A large organization of plastic surgeons in the USA.

Analyze: Closely study or research something.

Anorexia nervosa: A kind of eating disorder characterized by a fear of gaining weight; those with anorexia try to become or remain underweight by depriving themselves of food or by exercising excessively.

Anti-anxiety medication: Medication to treat anxiety disorders; medication that alters the chemicals in a person's brain and can make a person feel calmer and happier.

Antidepressant medication: Medication to treat depression; medication that alters the chemicals in a person's brain to alleviate symptoms of depression.

Anxiety disorder: Constant feelings of worry, anxiety, or fear that interfere with a person's daily life.

Artificial sweeteners: Food additives that provides a sweet taste in place of actual sugar, while also providing few to no calories.

Athletic: Relating to sports; muscular, strong, in shape.

Atkins diet: Low-carb diet; foods like pasta, bread, soft drinks, and sweets cannot be eaten according to this diet.

Autoimmune disorder: A disease in which the body's immune system attacks healthy cells.

Beauty sick(ness): When women spend energy worrying about their appearance at the cost of focusing on things like their education, careers, family, and relationships.

Behaviors (behavioral habits): The way in which a person acts, or does something; a regular way of doing something, a routine.

Benign: Mild, not harmful.

Benzoyl peroxide: A medicine used to treat acne and other skin conditions.

Biased: An opinionated view. A biased person cannot see something as it really is.

Binge(ing): Indulging excessively on a substance for a short period of time, usually consuming a lot of food or alcohol quickly.

Binge eating disorder (BED): An eating disorder that involves binging (at least once a week for at least 3 months) without purging. Binges are described as excessive in terms of how much is eaten and they're experienced as uncontrollable.

Blogger: A person who writes for a blog, which is usually an online publication of some sort.

Blood cholesterol (*see cholesterol*): When the body has too much cholesterol, it can get stuck in the blood vessels and contribute to heart disease.

Body dysmorphic disorder (BDD): A body image disorder. People with BDD focus on their body's flaws and are preoccupied with trying to fix flaws that are usually not noticeable to other people.

Body image: How you think or feel about your body; how you view your physical self on a day-to-day basis.

Body mass index (BMI): A person's weight in kilograms divided by the square of their height in meters.

Body odor (BO): The different scents the human body gives off; can become unpleasant (or stinky) when sweat mixes with bacteria that are found naturally on the skin.

Body shaming: Putting another person down because of how their body looks.

#BoPo: A hashtag for body-positive posts on social media.

Body-positive movement: A social justice movement that focuses on the importance of all people having positive body images and valuing bodies of all sizes and shapes.

Botulinum toxin (Botox): A drug made from the toxins of *Clostridium botulinum* bacteria. This toxin is what causes botulism, but it can also have many medical and cosmetic uses such as improving the appearance of wrinkles.

Botulism: A serious illness caused by ingesting *Clostridium botulinum* bacteria through contaminated water or food.

Breast growth: The increase in breast size that occurs during puberty in response to hormone changes.

Breathing exercises: Exercises that include breath control and deep breathing as a way to calm oneself or practice mindfulness.

British Psychological Society: An organization that represents psychologists in the UK and strives to promote excellence and ethical practices in education, research, and the provision of psychological services.

Bulimia nervosa: An eating disorder that involves binging and then purging food.

Bully (tease): Tease or mess with someone; aim to make a person feel inferior.

Calorie(s) (*also see kilocalories*): A unit of measurement to assess the amount of energy in a certain food; a unit of measurement used to describe the energy potential of a substance.

Cami: Short for camisole; a sleeveless undershirt; a spaghetti-strapped tank top that's often wore under shirts and sometimes has a built-in bra.

Cancer: A disease that's caused by an uncontrolled growth of abnormal cells in a part of the body.

Carb loading: Meals with a lot of carbohydrates in them, like bread and pasta, to give the body energy quickly. Often used by athletes when they have a big race or game.

Carbohydrates (carbs): Organic compounds that are an easy source of energy; carbs can help improve athletic performance.

Cellulite: The appearance of lumps and dimples on the surface of the skin, usually present on the thighs, butt, hips, and stomach; can have a texture like "orange peel" or "cottage cheese."

Centered: Balanced or in tune with one's body.

Centers for Disease Control and Prevention (CDC): A national public health agency and institution in the USA.

Cognitive: Related to mental processes or thoughts.

Chocoholic: How a person who feels as though they're "addicted" to chocolate may describe themselves.

Cholesterol: A fatty substance that's carried around the body in the blood. There is "good" (high-density) and "bad" (low-density) cholesterol.

Classy: High-class or sophisticated.

Clitoris: A small, fleshy, erectile organ of the female reproductive system, found at the front end of the human vulva; the primary source of female sexual pleasure.

Commitment strategy: A strategy developed to help one stick with a goal: for example, telling people about your goals and asking for help in achieving them.

Compassion(ate) (also see self-compassion): Showing caring, understanding, and kindness to a person and/or the issues a person is dealing with.

Compulsive exercise: Exercise that feels like an obligation, not something enjoyed; exercise that a person feels is necessary, maybe more than once per day.

Constipation: Irregular or infrequent movement and emptying of the bowels; less-than-regular passage of stool/feces.

Cosmetics: Products relating to a person's appearance (for example, make-up).

Cosmetic surgery: A type of surgery performed to change and enhance a person's physical appearance.

Criticism (also see self-criticism): Disapproval or harsh judgment.

Culprit: The cause of something negative.

Dairy: Any and all products that contain milk (for example, cheese, yogurt, ice cream, butter).

Dense (density): compacted closely, usually in terms of substance; thick

Depressed (depression, depressing): The way a person feels when they simply cannot become happy, so they remain in a sad "funk" or mood; depression is also a mental health disorder when it's a lasting negative mood and/or outlook on life.

Dermal fillers: Substances that are put into the skin to get rid of wrinkles, make lips bigger, or get rid of scars and imperfections.

Dermatologist: A doctor who specializes in skin care.

Despair: A feeling of hopelessness or distress.

Dextrose: A type of sugar.

Diabetes: A condition where a person's body doesn't make any or makes too little of a certain hormone (insulin) (type 1 diabetes), or where the person's body can't process a certain kind of sugar (type 2 diabetes).

Diet: How or what a person eats; a specific plan of foods to be eaten either to lose weight or for medical reasons.

Dietician (*also see nutritionist*): An expert who studies food and nutrition. Dieticians teach people what to eat in order to have a healthy lifestyle and/or manage health problems related to illness and disease; formal schooling, training, and certification is required to be considered a dietician.

Eating disorder: A category of conditions/illnesses that involve troublesome eating habits that can lead to serious problems and even death.

Embarrassed (embarrassment): A feeling that a person gets when unwanted attention is focused on them, similar to shame, awkwardness, and self-consciousness.

Embodiment: The sense of "being in touch with" or "happily living in" your body.

Empower (empowering): Encourage, support, or make a person feel more confident in themselves and their abilities.

Energy: The strength and activity you're able to experience, derived from the number of calories consumed.

Enhance (enhancements): Increase or upgrade something, or make improvements.

Evaluate: Judge or analyze something.

Evidence-based information: Information that comes from research that uses a scientific method; information based on scientific evidence.

Exercise: A particular type of physical activity that's usually planned and purposeful.

Exertion: Physical or mental effort; extra work or strain involved in doing a task.

Fad: Something (like a diet, fashion, or make-up trend) that becomes widely popular, but the hype goes away quickly; short-lived popularity.

Fallopian tubes: A pair of tubes that extend from the ovaries to the uterus along which eggs are transported (only found in females).

Fashionable: Popular or stylish.

Fast (fast-tailed): A slang term used to describe girls perceived as overly sexual or immodest, especially at a young age; derogatory.

Fast food: Food that is designed to be ordered and obtained quickly. Typically, fast food is not particularly healthy because preparation speed is prioritized over food quality.

Fasting: Not eating or drinking all or some kinds of foods and drinks, sometimes for a religious observance, or for weight loss.

Fat: A type of nutrient that the body uses for "fuel" and to store energy.

Fat talk: Negative discussion about the body that typically occurs with peers (for example, "I'm so fat!").

Fiber: Food that isn't digested or absorbed by the body.

Filter: A technique that changes the look of an image, usually to refine and improve certain aspects of the image.

Fitness: How healthy or strong someone is, relating to exercise and being physically active.

Fitspiration: Words, images, and videos that are intended to serve as motivation or inspiration to improve health and fitness.

Flatter: Make a person appear more attractive (for example, a piece of clothing, or a new hairstyle); compliment someone in an insincere way.

Flexitarians: People who eat a mostly vegetarian diet, but are not rigid in their approach.

Folate: Folic acid; one of the B vitamins, which is found in food.

Food addiction: A food habit that a person may rely on, but that doesn't involve a chemical dependency (alcohol and drug addictions typically involve a chemical dependency). Food addiction isn't considered an eating disorder by psychologists.

Food restriction: Cutting out a significant portion of food (or food groups), usually for weight loss, or for a health concern (such as diabetes).

Functionality: The ability to perform and serve a specific purpose (for example, legs serve the purpose or function of walking and running).

Genes: The building blocks of heredity or how we inherit characteristics from our biological parents.

Genetically modified organisms (GMOs): Organisms that have been genetically modified using different (biological) engineering techniques.

Genitals: Male and female reproductive body parts (for men, this includes the penis, and for women, the vagina).

Graves' disease: An autoimmune disorder that causes hyperthyroidism, or an overactive thyroid.

Groom(ing): Clean up or make neat.

Gynecologist: A doctor who takes care of girls' and women's reproductive health.

Hangry: Being so hungry that a person becomes angry or irritable in some cases (angry+hungry= hangry).

Harassment (*also see sexual harassment*): Any type of behavior that can be seen as offensive, inappropriate, or hurtful to another person.

Healthy: Physical, mental, and emotional wellness; free from illness or disease.

Healthy media diet: A limited use of media or certain types of media. It often refers to parents putting restrictions on their children's screen time, in particular to ensure that it doesn't interfere with their children's sleep.

Heart disease: A heart condition where a passageway into the heart can be blocked, or something is wrong with the heart's muscles.

High-fructose corn syrup: A sweetener frequently used in commercially produced foods and drinks that is made from cornstarch as a cheaper alternative to sucrose (or other sugar products).

High-intensity interval training (HIIT): Exercise routines or workouts that involve alternating between nearly all-out exertion (for example, running as fast as you can) and lower exertion (for example, jogging) for intervals of a minute (or some other set times) each.

Highlight reel: A slang term for a quick summary of the most relevant high points of someone's life.

Hormones: Chemicals the body produces that alter and control bodily functions. For example, there are hormones that alter feelings of hunger, sleepiness, and even happiness.

Hygiene: Cleanliness; practicing cleanliness for health and proper body care.

Hyperthyroidism: A condition caused by an overactive thyroid; the thyroid gland produces too much thyroid hormone, which can speed up the body's metabolism, causing symptoms like unintentional weight loss and a rapid or irregular heartbeat.

Hypothyroidism: A condition caused by an underactive thyroid; the thyroid gland produces too little thyroid hormone, which can slow down the body's metabolism, causing symptoms like weight gain and fatigue.

Influencer (social media influencer): A popular and influential social media user; a person who is used to promote certain items to persuade others to buy the products.

Insecure (insecurities): Feeling unconfident, doubtful, or unsure of oneself.

Instincts: Natural tendencies; things a person may do without realizing why.

Intermittent fasting: Limiting food eaten overall by reducing what's eaten during certain periods of time in a day or week. For example, a person may eat regularly for 5 days a week and then eat relatively little for a couple of days a week, or a person may eat within a select window of time each day.

Internalize (internalizing): Take information that's outside of you and make it your own; believe a thought, attitude, or behavior of others and make it yours—usually without realizing it.

International Society of Aesthetic Plastic Surgery: An international group of surgeons with expertise in plastic and cosmetic surgery. The group promotes the sharing of information among medical professionals and the public.

Intuitive eating: The process of listening to the body's signals of hunger and fullness and eating what's appealing, satisfying, and healthy.

Invest (investment): Put time, money, or effort into something in order to gain something in return.

Ironic processing: A term that describes trying to clear your mind of something, which then has the opposite effect. For example, if you tell someone not to think about chocolate, they may end up thinking about it more than they would have if you hadn't told them not to.

Juice concentrate: Juice from fruit that is processed or filtered to remove water.

Juicing: Extracting the juice from fruits and vegetables to drink the nutrients. Juicing typically removes the fiber from fruits and vegetables.

Ketogenic (diet, keto diet): A high-fat and low-carbohydrate (carb) diet. This sort of diet typically allows eating vegetables that grow above ground, eggs, seafood, unprocessed meats, high-fat dairy products and berries.

Kilocalorie (kcal; *also see calorie*): A measurement of the energy value of food. A kilocalorie is another word for what is commonly called a calorie, so 1,000 calories is usually written as 1,000 kcal.

Kilogram (kg): A unit of measurement for mass. One kilogram is equal to 2.2 pounds and 0.16 stone.

Labia majora: The outer folding of the vulva, part of the female genitals.

Labia minora: The inner folding of the vulva, part of the female genitals.

Lifestyle: The way in which a person or group of people live; this can include their career, culture, social class, and interests. For example, the lifestyle of a celebrity and a school teacher may be very different.

Literacy (literate): The knowledge and understanding of a particular topic, subject, or field of study.

Macrobiotic eaters: Vegans who only eat unprocessed foods and sometimes fish; they also avoid sugar and refined oils.

Magnesium: A mineral that has many important functions in the human body.

Manipulate: Control or influence something, especially in order deceive or mislead someone.

Mayo Clinic: A world-famous non-profit medical academic and research hospital, originally in Minnesota but now with other locations as well, which also has an online database containing information about certain diseases and illnesses.

Media: Any form of mass communication, which includes broadcasting (such as cable television and streaming), the internet (such as social media), and publications like newspapers (such as the *New York Times*).

Media literacy: Knowledge and understanding of the media, how and why it functions the way it does, or how to interpret information available in the media.

Meditation: A technique aimed to train the mind to be calm.

#MeToo: A movement started by celebrities against sexual harassment and unwanted sexual contact.

Meme: A funny, popular image or video that's widely spread and shared online—especially on social media.

Menstrual blood: The blood and tissue of the uterine lining that passes out of the vagina during menstruation.

Menstruation (menstrual period, period, menses): The process of expelling blood and tissue of the uterine lining from the vagina; first occurs for girls during puberty and ends after menopause. Menstruation pauses temporarily when women are pregnant, and loss of menses is usually a signal that a pregnancy has occurred.

Mental health: A person's condition in relation to psychological and emotional well-being.

Metabolism: The chemical processes that take place within the body that are essential to keep us alive.

Micronutrients: Vitamins and minerals that are needed to keep the body healthy, usually found in food.

Mindfulness: A practice of being aware of oneself and one's thoughts, feelings, physical body and physical surroundings.

Mindless eating: To eat something without enjoying the process of eating; sometimes eating without even being hungry, out of boredom.

Minerals: Solid substances that occur in nature.

Minimally invasive cosmetic treatments: Cosmetic treatments that are usually very easy to perform and don't require a lot of recovery time after they're finished; usually refers to substances injected into the face (for example, Botox) to minimize the appearance of wrinkles.

Misbeliefs: Misconceptions; wrong beliefs or misunderstandings, based on wrong information or an error in thinking or judgment.

Moderation: A middle ground or balance in behavior; not having too much or too little of something.

Motivate (motivation): Encourage someone to do something; feel inspired or eager to do something.

Muscular: Relating to muscles; having strong, or well-developed muscles.

My Plate: The US government's description of what to eat if we're trying to be healthy; it includes a focus on fruits and vegetables as approximately half of all foods eaten.

Myths: Stories or explanations that are sometimes passed on by communities to explain things that are not well understood.

National Eating Disorder Association: An American non-profit organization focused on eating disorder prevention and treatment, as well as education regarding eating disorders, weight, and body image.

Natural supplement: A type of dietary supplement that contains one or more plant-based products. Supplements can affect health but are not regulated by the US Food and Drug Administration (USFDA).

Negative: Not positive, desirable, or optimistic. A negative statement may be a statement of refusal.

Nipple: The colored part of the middle of the breast, often pink, tan, brown, or black, where milk comes out of to feed babies following a pregnancy.

No Mirror Movement: Originally, a group of dancers who wanted to change how women think about their bodies by avoiding use of mirrors. They focus on teaching mindfulness, self-care, and body acceptance as part of the experience of learning dance. This movement has been adopted by others who are interested in improving body image by reducing body scrutiny.

Non-profit organization: An organization that has a goal to provide aid or services and to contribute to an important cause. These organizations don't aim to make money, and any money that they obtain through donations or fundraising is used to further their organization's goals.

Nourish(ment): Food and other substances necessary for health and development.

Nutrition: The process of obtaining the components of food that are needed to support health.

Nutritional value: The amount of different nutrients in a particular food.

Nutritionist: A professional who studies food and nutrition. They teach people what to eat in order to have a healthy lifestyle and/or manage health problems related to illness and disease. A legal certification is not required to be considered a nutritionist.

Nutritious: Describes types of foods that are good for the body and likely to improve health.

Ovo-lacto vegetarians: Vegetarians who do eat eggs and drink milk.

Organic food: Food that is grown without the use of pesticides or other artificial substances.

Orthorexia: An overconcern with healthy eating that can be psychologically damaging. Although it is not a clinical diagnosis, orthorexia is often described as an eating disorder.

Overweight: Above what is considered a normal weight for a person's height by the medical community.

Pad (menstrual pad; sanitary napkin): An absorbent pad worn in the underwear by women and girls when they are having their period.

Paleo diet: Sometimes referred to as the caveman diet; a type of diet that's based on foods similar to what might have been eaten during the Paleolithic era (approximately 2.5 million–10,000 years ago). A paleo diet typically includes fruits, vegetables, lean meats, fish, nuts, and seeds.

Paralysis: The inability to move or feel a part of the body, or the entire body, due to an injury, illness, or poison.

Pediatrician: A doctor who deals with the health and wellness of children, usually aged 17 years and younger.

Percentile: The rank at which a person compares to other people in a given group; for example, it could be used to indicate how a person compares in height to other people of the same age and gender. (If your height is in the 70% percentile this means you're taller than, or as tall as, 70% of other people of the same age and gender.)

Period underwear: Reusable underwear with a leak-resistant lining to absorb blood during menstruation.

Personality: The sum of traits that makes up a person's character; a person's non-physical identity.

Pescatarian: A person who doesn't eat meat but eats fish; a type of vegetarian.

Pesticides: Chemicals used for killing bugs and other organisms that can be harmful to plants (typically plants grown for food) and should not be consumed by people.

Photoshop: A type of software used to alter photographs; digitally change an image using a program such as Adobe Photoshop.

Physical activity: Any kind of movement of the body.

Physical dependency: When the body depends on a substance to continue to function, such as a drug that creates a dependency, and discontinuing use of it would result in serious and unpleasant withdrawal symptoms.

Pornography: Printed or digital imagery or text containing sexually explicit content.

Portray (portrayal): Represent or show something/someone in a specific way.

Positive: Confident, optimistic, happy, or good.

Positive body image: Favorable opinions about the body, body acceptance, respect for the body, taking care of the body, and rejecting unrealistic standards of physical beauty.

Potassium: A type of mineral found in food that's good for the body; it helps with normal muscle growth and helps maintain water in the body.

Presentation (*also see self-presentation*): How a person shows themselves to the world.

Preservative: Something put into food to make it last longer and not spoil as quickly as a natural or unpreserved food.

Primping: Lightly grooming or tidying up; usually fixing up a person's hair or make-up.

Processed food: Food that's altered before people eat it. Processed foods usually have a lot of sugar, salt, and possibly fats added to them to improve their taste.

Proportions (body proportions): The relation of parts, in comparison to other parts or the whole of something (for example, proportions of the eyes in comparison to the lips or the whole face).

Protein: An important nutrient needed to help and protect various parts of the body including bones, muscles, cartilage, and skin.

Psychological disorders: A wide range of mental health conditions that affect mood, thinking, and behavior. Psychological disorders include eating disorders, depression, and anxiety.

Psychologist: A scientist who studies the human mind, including how people think, feel, and behave. Some psychologists provide therapy to help people talk through their problems or mental health disorders.

Puberty: The physical and hormonal changes that lead a child's body to grow into an adult body; this process is marked by the development of secondary sex characteristics (like breasts, pubic hair, and facial hair) and the ability to reproduce sexually (have babies).

Pubic hair: Body hair that appears on the genitals or in the genital regions during puberty.

Purging: Any means of ridding the body of food eaten; it can include taking medication that leads one to vomit or have diarrhea, or exercising extensively.

Realistic (*also see unrealistic*): Truthful, attainable, or reasonable.

Regimen: A kind of plan that may involve a medical treatment, a diet, or a general lifestyle change.

Research scientist (researcher; scientist): A person who has experience in, is considered an expert in, and studies a specific topic related to science.

Respect: Hold in high esteem or deep admiration.

Revealing: Showing more of something than usual; for example, revealing clothes show more of a person's body or a part of the body than usual.

Salicylic acid: An anti-inflammatory medication that treats acne and other skin conditions.

Salt: A mineral also known as sodium chloride; it is used to preserve foods and make foods taste better.

Sarcasm: Making a comment or joke in an ironic tone; usually the comment or joke doesn't match the person's tone or the words they're saying.

Saturated fat: A type of fat found in most dairy and meat products; a less healthy fat than unsaturated fat.

Savoring: Eating or drinking and enjoying the experience completely.

Science (scientific evidence): The study of the world learned by observations and experiments, usually by trained professionals (scientists).

Screen time: The amount of time spent using an electronic device, such as a phone, tablet, computer, or television.

Self-acceptance: The attitude of being comfortable with yourself, the good and the bad, without wanting to change for the approval of others.

Self-care: Taking care of yourself physically, emotionally, and mentally, especially during stressful times.

Self-compassion: Being understanding, patient, and kind to yourself, especially when feeling dissatisfied with your appearance, thoughts, or behaviors.

Self-conscious (*also see insecure*): Uncomfortable about yourself; nervous, tense, or shy.

Self-criticism: A person's negative view of themself.

Self-presentation: How people present themselves to others to create a certain narrative about themselves, and how they want other people to view them.

Sexting (sext): Sending sexually suggestive/explicit photos or text messages (sexts) to another person.

Sexual harassment: Inappropriate sexual behavior or language that is rude, hurtful, and unwelcome. Sexual harassment may include unwanted physical contact and assault.

Shaming: Embarrassing or putting down; making someone feel bad about a characteristic that they possess (or lack).

Social circle: A group of people socially connected in one form or another; for example, a small group of friends within a bigger group of friends would both be considered social circles.

Social comparison: When a person compares themselves with other people to determine their worth in some respect, or as a way to see how they measure up against them.

Social media: Social websites and electronic applications (apps) that allow people to socialize, and to create and share content with others within a digital, social network.

Society: A large group of people living together within a community.

Soda: A sweet, carbonated drink sometimes called soda pop (or just "pop").

Software: The digital programs and operations within an electronic device (such as a cell phone, computer, or games console).

Stigmatize: Judge someone as less worthy because they have a particular quality or circumstance; regard someone with disapproval because of a feature such as their body size, gender, race, or religion.

Stress: A state of physical, mental, or emotional strain usually caused by struggling to deal with a difficult situation.

Stressed: In a state of stress.

Stretch marks: Marks on the body that typically develop due to quick gains or losses in weight; most women and men have some stretch marks.

Stylist: A person who dresses someone up or does their make-up and hair in a stylish, professional manner.

Sugar: A sweet-tasting nutrient that's often desired and added to a lot of different foods to improve their taste.

Superficial: Shallow or surface level; not deep or meaningful.

Sweat glands: Tissue structures within the skin that secretes sweat out onto the surface of the skin.

Tampon: A shaped, soft cloth-like material inserted into the vagina to absorb menstrual blood.

Tax: A required added cost to a product such as a clothing purchase.

Technique: A specific, often skillful way of doing something.

Toiletries: Products used to clean the body (hygiene products) such as soap, toothpaste, and washcloths.

Trashy: Considered poor quality, low brow, or unsophisticated.

Tummy tuck: Also known as an abdominoplasty, a procedure that removes fat and skin from the abdomen (stomach) and repairs the abdominal muscles to create a firm, flat look to the abdomen.

US Food and Drug Administration (USFDA): A national federal agency that's responsible for the safety of food, medical drugs, and cosmetic products that humans and pets consume and/or use. USFDA doesn't monitor or control products such as vitamins and supplements.

Underweight: Below-normal weight for a person's height and age.

Unhealthy: Harmful to one's health.

Unhygienic (*also see hygiene*): unclean (not clean); not taking care of your body in a proper way.

Unnatural: Artificial or man-made.

Unprocessed foods: Whole foods; foods that aren't changed before they're eaten, like grains, fruits, and vegetables.

Unrealistic: Unreasonable; very difficult or impossible to do or obtain.

Unsaturated fat: A particular kind of fat (for example, the fat found in some fish); considered healthier than saturated fat.

Unspecified feeding or eating disorder: Eating habits that can disrupt a person's life and can lead to drastic weight gain or weight loss. A clinical eating disorder diagnosis that applies to individuals who aren't considered to have anorexia, bulimia, or binge eating disorder.

Uterine lining: The inner layer of the uterus.

Uterus: An internal female sex organ, the growth site for fetuses (babies) before they're born; it contains the uterine lining that's expelled during menstruation.

Vagina: The inner canal of the female genitals, leading to the uterus; the internal organ of the female genitals.

Vegan: A person who eats a specific diet that doesn't include any meat or dairy products.

Vegetarian: A person who eats a specific diet that doesn't include meat or products made with meat (chicken, chicken broth, pork, fish, beef).

Vitamins: Important elements found in foods that contribute to health and are sometimes taken in pill form.

Vulnerable: Feeling unsafe, unprotected, or overly exposed.

Vulva: External organs of the female genitalia; includes the labia minora, labia majora, clitoris, and other glands and tissue.

Water retention: When fluid builds up inside the body; a common symptom is swelling in the hands and feet. Sometimes called fluid retention or edema.

Waxing: Getting rid of unwanted hair by using hot wax (usually on a person's legs, underarms, face, or pubic area).

Weight stigma (weight bias/weight-based discrimination): When a person is viewed unfavorably or mistreated because they are overweight. For example, a person may be assumed to be lazy or addicted to junk food, just because they have a larger body.

Weight Watchers: A popular weight-loss program that involves a points system attached to foods, with the goal of losing weight and maintaining weight loss. Endorsed by Oprah Winfrey and other celebrities.

Well-being: A person's state of comfort and health.

Withdrawal: Unpleasant and potentially dangerous physical and mental symptoms that occur when stopping or reducing intake of a drug that a person has become dependent on.

World Health Organization (WHO): An agency of the United Nations that aims to address international public health issues.

Yoga: Hindu spiritual practice that includes breath control, meditation, and performing specific bodily postures, widely practiced for health and relaxation.

Yo-yo dieting: When a person loses weight, then gains weight, and then loses weight again, usually from extreme or inconsistent dieting, sometimes called weight-cycling.

INDEX

ACKNOWLEDGEMENTS

This book has been a collaborative effort. When I've described my goals in writing this book to my research assistants, my colleagues, my friends, my family, and even young girls I don't know particularly well, so many people have been willing to help in whatever way they can. It is inspiring to know many girls and women who are passionate about discussing issues pertaining to body image – issues that have often been difficult for them and they hope will be easier for the next generation of girls.

I am grateful to many people at Cambridge for believing in my vision, being generous with resources to bring this project to fruition, and being so incredibly supportive. Sarah Marsh co-parented this project and made it a pleasure every step of the way; without Sarah I am not sure *The Body Image Book for Girls* would exist today. Lori Handelman was an incredible editor, providing not just the necessary assistance with my punctuation (!) but much appreciated witty commentary throughout the book. Tim Oliver, our amazing illustrator, helped to bring this book to life. I know that many girls will open this book to see his drawings and only then decide to read a bit. Zoe Naylor provided a fabulous cover design (across many, many iterations) and an artistic vision for the entire book.

I am indebted to my colleagues and friends who have indulged my never-ending desire to discuss the issues I've written about in this book and even proof read many of the chapters, especially Kristin August, Laurie Bernstein (editor extraordinaire!), Jamie Dunaev, Meghan Gillen, Jennifer Rappaport, Amy Sepinwall, Katie Sibley, and Lorie Sousa.

I am thankful for my graduate and undergraduate students and research assistants who have been an invaluable source of help and encouragement, including Jo Abby Lods, Rachel Cefaratti, Allison Cooper, Erika Frick, Aaron Gomez, Molly Hartig, Kristin Kelley, Kristina Malson, and Miguel Orlina. And, I am especially appreciative of the research assistants who worked with me while I was drafting this book and did everything from reading drafts, helping with focus groups, and assisting with the glossary: Nana Amponsah, Emily Dangro, Lindsay Marx, Shannon McGlinn, and Samantha Quieti.

Of course, this book is for and about girls, and I am grateful to all of the girls who allowed me to interview them and who participated in focus groups to discuss book content, including Sophie Bergstrom, Libby Blum, Shadany Catalan, Danielle Chamberlain, Aseeli Coleman, Molly Conallen, Maya Grande, Rhys Hals, Melodie Healey, Lillian Hodges, Hannah Jarvis, Grace Markey, Elizabeth Meza, Ellie Newsome, Maya Oquendo, Abigail Oldham, Iryana Peralta, Christy Phillips, Abigail Rappaport, Hannah Rappaport, Osmary Rodea, Veronica Sanchez, Imogen Sharef, Riley Smith, Gabrielle Smyser, Zofia Soch, Ryan Sousa, Katie Stack, Whitney Taylor, Arlenys Veras, Elaysha Vereen, Maia Virgil, Josephine Wieland, and Sydney Williams.

And, finally, my family: My mom, Ar Monica Pribuss, the matriarch of our family, who embodies "girl power" in so many ways. My extended, loving, unconventional family, including Sayla Hart, for helping to organize focus groups with girls and believing that all girls deserve resources that enable empowerment. My husband, Dan Hart, for cheering me on, offering unwavering support and enthusiasm, and reading all of this more than once. And, my children, Charlie and Grace, who inspire everything I do.